D0146767

# Food Service Management
# by Checklist

# Food Service Management by Checklist
## A Handbook of Control Techniques

**Brother Herman E. Zaccarelli, C.S.C.**

*Assistant to the President*
*Director of Publications*
*California Culinary Academy*

**WILEY**

**John Wiley & Sons, Inc.**

New York  •  Chichester  •  Brisbane  •  Toronto  •  Singapore

Copyright © 1991 by California Culinary Academy

Published by John Wiley & Sons, Inc.

**Library of Congress Cataloging-in-Publication Data**

Zaccarelli, Herman E., 1931–
    Food service management by checklist : a handbook of control
techniques / Herman E. Zaccarelli.
    p.    cm.
    ISBN 0-471-53063-8
    1. Food service management.    I. Title.
TX611.3.M27Z33    1990
647.95'068—dc20

                                       90-12734
                                       CIP

Printed in the United States of America

91  92    10 9 8 7 6 5 4 3

# Foreword

Brother Herman Zaccarelli is known for his unique (some would say radical) approach to food service management education. He is a man of many "firsts," and in this book he again shows why he is at the forefront of educational programming in our field.

*Food Service Management by Checklist* is an outstanding addition to the body of food service management literature. I believe it is destined to take its place along with *Professional Cooking* and *Food for Fifty* as a management standard. This book may well revolutionize food service management for the operating professional. It is quick, hard-hitting, and, most importantly, comprehensive. It takes the traditional managerial process philosophy of Henri Fayol, which is so familiar to students of management thought, and adds those areas specific to our industry.

Brother Herman has written a book that is user friendly. I would expect no less from a man who has kept at the head of his field for so many years. He also has developed the most creative food service management book published in a decade. Use it, and, as I did, find a wealth of important information gathered for easy reference in one place, in usable order. Much of it you will apply immediately. Most of it will make you think. All of it will make you say, "I am better, sharper, and more able to face the challenges of my management position now." Thanks, Brother Herman, from all of us who, like you, hope to further the professionalism of hospitality management. You have done more than your part.

Joseph J. Cioch, Dean
*Hilton College of Hotel and Restaurant Management*
*University of Houston*

# Preface

Food service managers in commercial and institutional food service operations are busy people. They are responsible for the management and control of many resources and must, at the same time, be marketing experts who can satisfy (or exceed) the wants, needs, and expectations of the many internal and external constituencies they serve.

There is a wide body of information in the general discipline of management and more specifically within that of the hospitality industry. With some obvious exceptions, basic principles have been discovered which can be applied to the resolution of many of our problems. There are proven ways to help assure that we as food service managers optimize the attainment of financial and other established goals.

It is the thesis of this handbook that many busy professionals know but may not have the time to apply much of the information most helpful to them in the operation of food service programs. What is needed, therefore, is a fast and succinct way to be briefed upon these basic principles and to find ways to incorporate them into the way things are done.

*Food Service Management by Checklist: A Handbook of Control Techniques* explains a process and provides numerous specific examples of one way to address this issue. Many of us use checklists in our personal and professional lives. We jot important items on pieces of paper (where did I leave that scratch paper?), we make notes on our daily calendars, and we invent other ways to remember what needs to be done. A more formalized approach to this method can be helpful and is explored in this handbook.

This writer wishes to formally salute the dedicated, professional men and women who work many hours helping to serve humanity in our food service industry. The goals of this handbook will have been achieved if the information presented helps just a little to make their work easier and more organized. The purpose of this handbook will have been attained if our own managers are better pleased with our work and our guests (including students, residents, patients, and others in not-for-profit environments) receive better value from and more enjoyment of the meals served to them.

# Acknowledgments

The author expresses his deep gratitude to the following professionals who assisted by their counsel and constructive criticism to bring this book to fruition.

James M. Bedtke, M.B.A., President
Center for Marketing and Management
Winona, Minnesota

Thomas A. Bloom, Ph.D., President
California Culinary Academy
San Francisco, California

Joseph J. Circh, Ph.D., Dean
Conrad Hilton College of Hotel and Restaurant Management
University of Houston
Houston, Texas

Jeff Graves, M.A., Associate Professor
Conrad Hilton College of Hotel and Restaurant Management
University of Houston
Houston, Texas

Donald M. Jacobs, C.H.A., Executive Director–Hospitality Services
University of Pennsylvania
Philadelphia, Pennsylvania

Michael M. Lefever, Ph.D., Associate Dean
Conrad Hilton College of Hotel and Restaurant Management
University of Houston
Houston, Texas

Russell Pottle, President
Copy Plus
Duxbury, Massachusetts

Edward G. Sherwin, M.A., President-Elect
Council of Hotel, Restaurant, and Institutional Educators
Essex Community College
Baltimore, Maryland

Claire Thompson, Hospitality Editor
Professional, Reference, and Trade Division
John Wiley & Sons, Inc.
New York, New York

It is hoped that this book will assist our dedicated food service professionals in the continued development of their food service operations.

# Contents

# Introduction: All About Checklists

In the following information, you will discover basic principles helpful in developing and utilizing checklists for food service management. You will discover what they are, what topics they can cover, and how they can help you become more quickly aware of basic principles which can be helpful in long- and short-term management of your food service operation.

**What Is a Checklist?**

A checklist is, as the name implies, a listing of specific factors which are applicable to a process or to more specific procedures. Depending upon its format, a food service manager can use a checklist to identify what should be done, exactly how it should be done, by whom it should be done, and when it should be done, and to assess whether tasks are performed correctly. Checklists can be—and are—developed to review almost any activity within a food service organization.

**Why Use a Checklist?**

Food service managers may desire to utilize a checklist technique for several reasons:

- To serve as a training tool. Since a checklist specifies exact procedures which should be followed as an activity is undertaken, it provides a reminder of the points to be addressed as training for a specific task is developed and undertaken.

- To assist in supervision. A checklist can refresh the memory of a food service manager about specific procedures which should consistently be used.

- To serve as a judge when there are differences of opinion as to required procedures. Since the checklist indicates the correct way an activity is to be performed, it can resolve questions which may arise about required procedures.

- To serve as a control tool. If, for example, actual costs are not in line with those planned, checklists can be reviewed to assure that the way things are done is, in fact, the way things should be done.

- To help solve problems. Many problems are incurred because basic management principles are not applied. Food service managers can review principles on checklists to gain ideas about what may—or may not—be helpful in meeting daily challenges on the job.

1

## How Is a Checklist Developed?

Basically, a food service manager develops a checklist from careful consideration of procedures which should be used in the operation. A checklist is, in effect, the answer to questions such as "how should a cash register be operated?"; "how should product receiving be undertaken in our operation?"; "what activities must be undertaken as a new employee is oriented/inducted into our operation?" If it has been properly developed, a property's Standard Operating Procedures (SOP) Manual can be used as the basis for a checklist. Likewise, if one is available, a job breakdown (a tool used in job analysis to define exactly how work is to be done) can form the foundation for a checklist.

In addition to thinking about how a procedure is to be undertaken, the food service manager must also consider the exact purpose to be served by the checklist. For example, if it is to identify responsibilities for task performance, information about the name/position that is to be assigned a specific task must be addressed. If its purpose is to serve as a reminder about task performance, a simple "yes or no" format may be appropriate. If the checklist is to identify deficiencies in operations, a section applicable to follow-up recommendations might be helpful.

Frequently, a participative approach is most useful in developing a checklist. That is, the food service staff members who must undertake and supervise performance of the activity should be involved in checklist development. For example, if the checklist is to address product receiving activities, the receiving clerk, the immediate superior of this employee, and the department head with ultimate responsibility for the activity might all be involved in a "give and take" session to arrive at specific procedures to be utilized. (Consider, also, other benefits which can be derived from this participative technique: agreement/consensus about the "best" procedures can be developed, clarification of potential problems can be addressed, and affected employees can understand that the procedures which are used are their techniques rather than the management's.

## Who Has the Time?

Hopefully, some of the advantages of using a checklist are now recognized. However, when will a busy food service manager have the time to develop checklists (or even to modify those which are included later in this handbook)? It is obvious that one cannot stop producing and serving food until the checklists are developed. Several suggestions for addressing this issue include the following:

- Set aside some time each day to consider the most significant problems which confront your food service operation. What exactly is the problem? What are alternative ways to resolve it? What specific techniques can help in the resolution task? Who needs to be involved? By when must significant elements in the resolution plan be undertaken? The answers to these and related questions can help to identify specific elements which can be incorporated into a checklist. Give this a try: Pass around the first draft of the checklist being developed to others affected by the problem. Fine-tune it with their responses. You are likely to see that a usable checklist that addresses a specific issue will evolve in this process and that the checklist can be useful for addressing future, similar issues.

- Make assignments. If, for example, you have periodic training problems, ask one or more attendees to bring a brief checklist to the session which indicates standard procedures for how a task should be done or how a project should be evaluated. The content of the checklist can, then, be a focus of the training session. It can be revised as a result of the discussion and can yield a document which was actually developed by affected staffmembers for their own use on their own job.

- As you read chapters in a book or trade journal articles in a magazine, make a brief outline (list!) of the basic principles. You will see that these can be readily translated into a checklist for your operation which addresses the issues noted in the chapter/trade journal article.

Hopefully, the many checklists in this handbook can be modified for use in your food service operation. Use ones of specific interest to you as a basis for analysis and discussion by your staff. Is the topic addressed by the checklist applicable to your operation? How, if at all, must it be modified to more specifically fit your needs (this question addresses both the content and format of the checklist)? Perhaps two or more checklists can be combined, or you may be able to insert information from other in-house sources.

When developing checklists, you will find it helpful to recall a basic management principle: an assignment is not given until a time restraint is established. In other words, if you decide to work on the development of a checklist "when you get around to it," you will likely find that the task is never accomplished. Rather, establish a self-imposed goal (we will develop one checklist per week, month, or other time period). Allocate time as necessary to stay within the time limitations imposed by this goal. You will likely find that checklists can be developed without sacrificing the management efforts needed for all of your other important tasks.

## How to Use This Handbook

It is doubtful that all of the checklists which follow can be used by every manager of a food service operation. The vast range of differences in goals, procedures, available equipment, and so on make universal application of any checklist an improbability. These checklists do, however, provide examples of many techniques that can be addressed in a checklist format and they also illustrate various formats which can be used.

There are two basic ways that you can work with the checklists in this handbook. First, you may wish to read the information, in sequence, from cover-to-cover just as you would almost any other book. In this way, you will get a detailed idea about its contents and, hopefully, obtain some new information in the process. Alternatively, you may wish to utilize the detailed table of contents to locate issues of specific concern to you. Then, you can turn to the applicable pages and study the specific checklist(s) of most interest. Busy food service managers will find this latter approach more useful. In other words, they will use, rather than read, the handbook. However, the former approach (read the material in sequence) can also be helpful for new managers and for those undertaking a career development program in which basic background information is needed to form the foundation for further study.

Different checklists in this handbook can be used for specific purposes. For example, several (see those in Part Two) can be used to specifically question whether standard operating procedures are—or should be—in use. Others (see those in Part Four) provide a listing of general principles; the task of the reader is to assess whether—and how—they are applicable to a specific food service department. In effect, the principles listed in the checklists will need to be applied as the management decision-making process evolves. Still others (see several in Part Six) are a combination of the above; they provide information about specific operating procedures and, at the same time, note specific principles which may be helpful in the management task.

# Part I | Checklists for Basic Food Service Management Functions

# 1. Basic Management: Principles of Planning

| Factor | Not Applicable | Status | | | |
|---|---|---|---|---|---|
| | | Acceptable | In Process | Need to Do | Comments |
| 1. Managers are fully aware of the organization's mission statement; it is written and distributed. | | | | | |
| 2. The food service department has a long-range plan. | | | | | |
| 3. The food service department has a one-year (business) plan. | | | | | |
| 4. Food service managers develop weekly (or other) schedules for all employees. | | | | | |
| 5. The department has a reasonable financial plan (operating budget). | | | | | |
| 6. The organization has a timely marketing plan. | | | | | |
| 7. Policies are available to address all of the most recurring concerns, are included in an applicable handbook, and have been distributed to all staff members; policies are consistently applied. | | | | | |
| 8. Objectives are specific and measurable. | | | | | |

| Factor | Not Applicable | Status | | | |
|---|---|---|---|---|---|
| | | Acceptable | In Process | Need to Do | Comments |
| 9. Procedures are in place to allocate resources according to priority objectives. | | | | | |
| 10. A monitoring system is in place to assess progress toward obtaining objectives. | | | | | |
| 11. An objective problem-solving approach is used to determine the best way to move toward objectives. | | | | | |
| 12. Progress toward goal attainment is consistently and objectively evaluated. | | | | | |
| 13. Forecasts of production requirements are made and used in planning for daily operations. | | | | | |
| 14. Time is set aside for formal planning. | | | | | |
| 15. Plans, once developed, are implemented. | | | | | |
| 16. All affected persons are involved in the planning process. | | | | | |

| Factor | Not Applicable | Status | | | |
|---|---|---|---|---|---|
| | | Acceptable | In Process | Need to Do | Comments |
| 17. Coordinating activities helps assure that persons in other departments are involved in the planning process. | | | | | |
| 18. Planning begins at the top of the department (organization) and responsibilities flow through the department as needed. | | | | | |
| 19. Specific action plans are utilized to implement broad plans. | | | | | |
| 20. Procedures to implement change as necessary are included in the planning process. | | | | | |
| 21. Analysis is done to help assure that plans are cost-effective. | | | | | |
| 22. Planning precedes other management functions (organizing, coordinating, supervising, etc.) | | | | | |
| 23. Procedures to communicate plans are developed and implemented. | | | | | |
| 24. An objective process is utilized to evaluate alternative plans. | | | | | |

| Factor | Not Applicable | Status | | | |
|---|---|---|---|---|---|
| | | Acceptable | In Process | Need to Do | Comments |
| 25. Time and required information are made available to those with responsibility for planning. | | | | | |
| 26. Persons who are affected by plans are allowed to contribute to plan development. | | | | | |
| 27. When practical, planning is flexible. | | | | | |

# 2. Basic Management: Principles of Organizing

| Factor | Procedure | | Corrective Action | Requirements |
|---|---|---|---|---|
| | In Place | Not Done | | |
| 1. There is a formal flow of authority and communication throughout the food service department and to other departments within the organization. | | | | |
| 2. A timely and accurate organization chart for the food service department and the entire property exists. | | | | |
| 3. Unity of command is practiced; each employee has only one boss. | | | | |
| 4. Similar activities are grouped together to form work sections. | | | | |
| 5. Similar tasks are grouped together to form positions. | | | | |
| 6. Line positions (the "chain of command") and staff positions (specialists who provide advice/counsel to those in the line) have been established; staff personnel provide help to but do not make decisions for line employees. | | | | |

| Factor | Procedure | | Corrective Action | Requirements |
|---|---|---|---|---|
| | In Place | Not Done | | |
| 7. Each supervisor/manager can effectively supervise the number of personnel assigned to him/her. | | | | |
| 8. There is clear functional authority; managers in each department know how, if at all, managers in other departments can impose authority upon them. | | | | |
| 9. The food service department is flexible; the organization can be changed as necessary to accommodate the fast-paced change of the property/organization/industry. | | | | |
| 10. The department is organized to promote efficiency. | | | | |
| 11. The "chain of command" allows authority (power) to be delegated. | | | | |

# 3. Basic Management: Principles of Coordinating

| Factor | Procedure | | Corrective Action | Requirements |
|---|---|---|---|---|
| | In Place | Not Done | | |
| 1. Each manager in the food service department has the authority (power) necessary to be effective. | | | | |
| 2. Top-level managers delegate necessary authority as work is assigned to subordinates. | | | | |
| 3. All personnel realize that responsibility (obligation) cannot be delegated. | | | | |
| 4. The authority exists at some level within the food service department to make any decision within its mission. | | | | |
| 5. Channels of communication allow free transmittal of messages up, down and across the organizational structure. | | | | |
| 6. All departments within the organization work in harmony with each other. | | | | |
| 7. Managers make use of information gained informally through the employee grapevine. | | | | |

| Factor | Procedure | | Corrective Action | Requirements |
| --- | --- | --- | --- | --- |
| | In Place | Not Done | | |
| 8. Meetings are held on a frequent basis with employees in the food service department to resolve problems and plan future activities. | | | | |
| 9. The manager of the food service department is on an equal level with other department managers and participates in "executive council" meetings. | | | | |

*Note:* In many respects the management task of coordinating is similar to that of communicating; see Checklist 29, Part V (page 117) in this handbook.

# 4. Basic Management: Principles of Staffing

| Factor | Procedure | | Corrective Action | Requirements |
|---|---|---|---|---|
| | In Place | Not Done | | |
| 1. Jobs are defined in terms of tasks which must be performed. | | | | |
| 2. Personal qualities needed to adequately perform required tasks have been considered and are written in current and accurate job specifications. | | | | |
| 3. All possible sources of job applicants are considered as vacancies are filled. | | | | |
| 4. Basic selection tests are utilized when practical to assess experiences of job applicants. | | | | |
| 5. Job application forms are used to collect information about applicants; forms which are used are in compliance with current Equal Opportunity Commission requirements. | | | | |
| 6. Screening devices are used to assess applicants for positions. | | | | |

| Factor | Procedure | | Corrective Action | Requirements |
|---|---|---|---|---|
| | In Place | Not Done | | |
| 7. Early job experiences affect an employee's relationship with the food service department; an effective orientation program (see Checklist 31, Part V, page 127) is in use. | | | | |
| 8. Effective employee training programs are developed and in use. | | | | |
| 9. Formal employee appraisal programs are effective and included as an integral part of staffing activities (see Checklist 25, Part V, page 108). | | | | |
| 10. Creative staffing patterns help to retain under- and over-employed staff members. | | | | |
| 11. There is an ongoing program of management development within the food service department (see Checklist 28, Part V, page 116). | | | | |
| 12. Food service managers are involved in decisions about transfers, promotions, and demotions which are part of the staffing process. | | | | |

| Factor | Procedure | | Corrective Action | Requirements |
|---|---|---|---|---|
| | In Place | Not Done | | |
| 13. In large food service organizations, there is a harmonious working relationship between the food service department and the staff personnel division. | | | | |
| 14. Supervisors who will be responsible for managing the work of new employees are involved in the selection decision. | | | | |

# 5. Basic Management: Principles of Directing

| Factor | Procedure | | Corrective Action | Requirements |
|---|---|---|---|---|
| | In Place | Not Done | | |
| 1. Departmental goals are, to the extent practical, meshed with those of staff members. | | | | |
| 2. Staff members know what is expected of them; standards for the quality and quantity of work performance have been established. | | | | |
| 3. Training programs for experienced staff are ongoing. | | | | |
| 4. Procedures for issuing orders relate to the quality of work expected. | | | | |
| 5. Food service managers use effective delegation principles (see Checklist 30, Part V, page 125). | | | | |
| 6. Food service managers use effective techniques of employee motivation (see Checklist 26, Part V, page 111). | | | | |
| 7. Food service managers use effective procedures for employee discipline (see Checklist 23, Part V, page 104). | | | | |

| Factor | Procedure | | Corrective Action | Requirements |
|---|---|---|---|---|
| | In Place | Not Done | | |
| 8. Orders which are given are reasonable, understood by the employee, and compatible with the tasks that the employee should perform. | | | | |
| 9. The "leadership style" which is used to direct the work of employees is appropriate to that of staff being directed. | | | | |
| 10. Food service managers recognize that their attitudes toward work and employees affect the attitudes and work of subordinate staff. | | | | |
| 11. Food service managers treat all employees fairly and consistently. | | | | |
| 12. Employee ideas are solicited and, when possible, incorporated into ongoing work procedures. | | | | |
| 13. Food service managers show their appreciation to employees as work is done effectively. | | | | |

| Factor | Procedure | | Corrective Action | Requirements |
|---|---|---|---|---|
| | In Place | Not Done | | |
| 14. Food service managers do not resist change except when appropriate; a process to implement new procedures is in place (see Checklist 22, Part V, page 102). | | | | |
| 15. Food service managers are able to communicate effectively with staff members (see Checklist 29, Part V, page 117). | | | | |

*Note*: Principles of directing are, in many ways, similar to those of supervising. The latter is the topic of Part V in this handbook.

# 6. Basic Management: Principles of Controlling

| Factor | Procedure | | Corrective Action | Requirements |
|---|---|---|---|---|
| | In Place | Not Done | | |
| 1. Performance standards indicating what things should be like in the absence of a problem have been established. | | | | |
| 2. Performance standards define desired quality and quantity levels. | | | | |
| 3. Control procedures are in place for food, beverage, labor, and sales income procedures. | | | | |
| 4. Actual performance is assessed in a manner consistent with standard performance. | | | | |
| 5. Allowable tolerance (variance levels) are established for each performance standard. | | | | |
| 6. Food service managers take corrective action when actual performance does not meet the standards (including variances) which have been established. | | | | |
| 7. Results of corrective action are evaluated to assure that problems have been resolved. | | | | |

| Factor | Procedure | | Corrective Action | Requirements |
|---|---|---|---|---|
| | In Place | Not Done | | |
| 8. Control systems are available to indicate problems on a timely basis. | | | | |
| 9. Control standards are objectively assessed. | | | | |
| 10. Control standards are flexible. | | | | |
| 11. Controls are "worth more than they cost." | | | | |
| 12. Operating budgets are used as a control tool. | | | | |
| 13. Corrective actions establish priorities to resolve problems that are the most important (costly) to the food service operation. | | | | |
| 14. Control systems reflect plans which have been developed. | | | | |
| 15. Control sets a priority focus on those factors judged most strategic to attainment of departmental goals. | | | | |
| 16. The control system utilized is periodically reviewed. | | | | |

| Factor | Procedure | | Corrective Action | Requirements |
|---|---|---|---|---|
| | In Place | Not Done | | |
| 17. Food service managers recognize that one problem can have "spin-off" effects on other areas of the department/organization; evaluation procedures address this issue. | | | | |
| 18. Food service managers recognize that "preventive" control procedures are more effective than imposing controls after things go wrong. | | | | |

# 7. Basic Management: Principles of Evaluation

| Factor | Procedure | | Corrective Action | Requirements |
|---|---|---|---|---|
| | In Place | Not Done | | |
| 1. Food service managers are aware that evaluation is necessary to measure the extent to which departmental goals are attained. | | | | |
| 2. Evaluation is included as an integral process in control procedures. | | | | |
| 3. Employees are evaluated through a formal performance appraisal process (see Checklist 25, Part V, page 108). | | | | |
| 4. The effectiveness of training is evaluated to assess its worth to the food service department and the employee. | | | | |
| 5. Evaluation is assigned a priority in the management of the food service operation; formal time is allowed/scheduled for the task. | | | | |
| 6. Existing departmental mission statements, long-range and business plans, and other tools of planning are periodically evaluated to assess whether changes are necessary. | | | | |

| Factor | Procedure | | Corrective Action | Requirements |
|---|---|---|---|---|
| | In Place | Not Done | | |
| 7. Input from the guests (including patients, residents, etc.) is solicited and utilized to help evaluate the food service department. | | | | |
| 8. As a result of evaluation, organizational resources available to the department are reallocated. | | | | |
| 9. Evaluation is done on a timely basis. | | | | |
| 10. Some evaluation techniques are objective (not subjective) to help assure the accuracy of evaluation results. | | | | |

# Part II | Product Control Procedures

# 8. Product Purchasing

| Factor | Procedure | | Corrective Action | Requirements |
|---|---|---|---|---|
| | In Place | Not Done | | |
| 1. Purchase specifications which define minimum quality requirements are available for all of the most expensive food products purchased. | | | | |
| 2. All purchasing procedures are written in a timely operating procedures manual. | | | | |
| 3. One manager is responsible for all purchasing decisions (a centralized purchasing system is in use). | | | | |
| 4. An in-house record is kept of all purchase agreements (item, quantity, purchase price, etc.). | | | | |
| 5. Input from suppliers is solicited about ways to improve the purchasing system. | | | | |
| 6. The quantity available in storage is considered when purchase quantities are determined. | | | | |

| Factor | Procedure | | Corrective Action | Requirements |
|---|---|---|---|---|
| | In Place | Not Done | | |
| 7. When practical, prices are solicited with and without delivery charges, so that the cost efficiency, if any, of pickup at the supplier's facility can be assessed. | | | | |
| 8. The right quality (not necessarily highest quality) product is purchased depending upon product use. | | | | |
| 9. When product prices increase, the continued need for the product is assessed. | | | | |
| 10. Speculation about price changes is undertaken by management staff—not by purchasing employees. | | | | |
| 11. Products are purchased in the most cost-effective purchase unit size. | | | | |
| 12. Centralized buying and one-stop shopping methods are investigated, when applicable, for use at the property. | | | | |
| 13. When practical, price quotations are solicited for products of similar quality from several suppliers. | | | | |

| Factor | Procedure | | Corrective Action | Requirements |
|---|---|---|---|---|
| | In Place | Not Done | | |
| 14. When practical, promotional discounts are taken on selected products. | | | | |
| 15. Production staff and guests (consumers) are polled about their preferences for products which are to be purchased. | | | | |
| 16. Negotiation principles are used in efforts to reduce purchase prices without sacrificing quality requirements. | | | | |
| 17. If there is a problem paying a bill, the matter is promptly discussed with the supplier. | | | | |
| 18. Payment terms are negotiated *after* the price is agreed upon. | | | | |
| 19. Specific policies regarding the use of petty cash funds for product purchases are in place. | | | | |
| 20. Prior experience with suppliers is used to assess whether a supplier relationship should be continued. | | | | |

| Factor | Procedure | | Corrective Action | Requirements |
|---|---|---|---|---|
| | In Place | Not Done | | |
| 21. The technical ability of the supplier's staff is a factor in determining which supplier(s) should be utilized. | | | | |
| 22. Procedures are in place to help assure that a supplier's invoice/ statement is not paid twice. | | | | |
| 23. Unless the employee is the manager/owner, the same individual does not normally purchase and receive products. | | | | |
| 24. Make/buy decisions are only assessed when alternative products are judged to be of equal quality. | | | | |
| 25. To the extent practical, all costs (both direct and indirect) are assessed as make/buy analyses are undertaken. | | | | |
| 26. Purchase decisions are always made on the basis of what is best for the company—not on what is best for the purchaser. | | | | |
| 27. A code of ethics relating to relationships with suppliers has been written and is in effect. | | | | |

| Factor | Procedure | | Corrective Action | Requirements |
|---|---|---|---|---|
| | In Place | Not Done | | |
| 28. A wide variety of resource material is available to help in the development of purchase specifications. | | | | |
| 29. Formal procedures are used to evaluate the effectiveness of the purchasing system. | | | | |
| 30. A formal system of keeping current with new products and new suppliers is in use. | | | | |
| 31. Procedures are in place to minimize the need for frequent expediting of emergency or rush orders. | | | | |
| 32. Products are purchased on a by-brand basis only when there is no other convenient standard which can be applied. | | | | |

# 9. Product Receiving

| Factor | Procedure | | Corrective Action | Requirements |
|---|---|---|---|---|
| | In Place | Not Done | | |
| 1. Someone has been trained to perform all required receiving tasks. | | | | |
| 2. Written quality specifications are available in the receiving area and are used as part of the receiving process. | | | | |
| 3. Receiving personnel are able to recognize the required quality of incoming products as dictated by the purchase specification. | | | | |
| 4. The duties of purchasing and receiving personnel are split; they are not done by the same employee (unless that person is the owner/ manager). | | | | |
| 5. Employees have been told about the importance of effective and careful product receiving. | | | | |
| 6. Employees with receiving duties are allowed time to perform them correctly. | | | | |
| 7. The receiving area is located near the delivery door. | | | | |

| Factor | Procedure | | Corrective Action | Requirements |
|---|---|---|---|---|
| | In Place | Not Done | | |
| 8. The amount of space allocated for receiving is ample to allow all products in a delivery to be inspected at one time. | | | | |
| 9. All necessary receiving equipment (including a receiving scale) is available in the receiving area. | | | | |
| 10. The receiving scale is accurate and is routinely verified for accuracy. | | | | |
| 11. The in-house record of products being purchased is available and is checked against incoming shipments at time of receiving. | | | | |
| 12. All incoming products are weighed, counted, or measured before the delivery invoice is signed. | | | | |
| 13. The delivery invoice is checked against the in-house record of purchase requirements before the invoice is signed. | | | | |
| 14. Receiving personnel know whom to contact when a receiving problem is observed. | | | | |

| Factor | Procedure | | Corrective Action | Requirements |
|---|---|---|---|---|
| | In Place | Not Done | | |
| 15. Hours during which products are received have been determined and made known to suppliers so that adequate time is available for the task. | | | | |
| 16. A Receiving Clerk's Daily Report or other form is used to summarize products received during a shift/day. | | | | |
| 17. After receiving tasks are completed, products are promptly removed to storage. | | | | |
| 18. Delivery personnel are allowed very limited access to back-of-house areas. | | | | |
| 19. All receiving documents are routed to food service management personnel before moving to the accounting department. | | | | |
| 20. Incoming products are placed behind/underneath existing products in inventory. | | | | |
| 21. Incoming products are dated to help in product rotation efforts. | | | | |

| Factor | Procedure | | Corrective Action | Requirements |
|---|---|---|---|---|
| | In Place | Not Done | | |
| 22. Incoming products are marked with the purchase price to aid in inventory valuation. | | | | |
| 23. Credit memos are always used when products are rejected and/or when products are on back-order (but still appear on the invoice). | | | | |
| 24. Portion control items are, on a routine but random basis, weighed to assure that portion size specifications are maintained. | | | | |
| 25. Ice, packaging material, cardboard casing, etc., are removed before products are weighed. | | | | |
| 26. Incoming products purchased by count (such as 96 count lemons) are counted on a routine but random basis. | | | | |
| 27. Suppliers are immediately notified of problems uncovered during delivery. | | | | |
| 28. The outside door is kept locked whenever possible; an audio signal is used to permit delivery personnel to indicate when they have arrived. | | | | |

| Factor | Procedure | | Corrective Action | Requirements |
|---|---|---|---|---|
| | In Place | Not Done | | |
| 29. A simple and practical method is used to verify product quality based upon standards established by the purchase specification. | | | | |
| 30. Management personnel with ultimate responsibility for purchasing and receiving routinely observe the receiving process. | | | | |
| 31. Receiving staff know and are alert to common ways that suppliers can substitute items of lower-than-desired quality. | | | | |

# 10. Product Storing and Issuing

| Factor | Procedure | | Corrective Action | Requirements |
|---|---|---|---|---|
| | In Place | Not Done | | |
| 1. Food service management know, at any point in time, the quantity of products which *should* be available in inventory. | | | | |
| 2. Food service management know, at any point in time, the quantity of items which *are* available in inventory. | | | | |
| 3. Unauthorized personnel are not allowed access to storage areas. | | | | |
| 4. All expensive items are kept under perpetual inventory records. | | | | |
| 5. All items in storage are marked with date of receipt and unit (or other) cost information. | | | | |
| 6. A physical count of items in inventory is taken at least monthly for accounting purposes (Cost of Goods Sold on Income Statement). | | | | |
| 7. Storage areas are lockable (or, at least, the most expensive inventory items are maintained in lockable areas). | | | | |

| Factor | Procedure | | Corrective Action | Requirements |
|---|---|---|---|---|
| | In Place | Not Done | | |
| 8. Items in work stations are placed under central inventory control at the end of each shift. | | | | |
| 9. Items which are under locked storage and are needed during a shift are retrieved by a management official. | | | | |
| 10. Storage areas are designed to help keep the area secure from unauthorized employee access. | | | | |
| 11. Food is rotated while in storage; items in storage the longest are issued first. | | | | |
| 12. Foods are stored at proper temperature levels.<br><br>a. Refrigerated items are kept below 40°F. | | | | |
| b. Dry storage areas range from 50°F to 70°F. | | | | |
| c. Frozen items are kept between 0°F and -10°F. | | | | |

| Factor | Procedure | | Corrective Action | Requirements |
|---|---|---|---|---|
| | In Place | Not Done | | |
| 13. Storage areas are kept clean; cleaning is scheduled and ongoing supervision is used to help assure that all required cleaning duties are consistently undertaken. | | | | |
| 14. There is effective ventilation in all storage areas. | | | | |
| 15. Rodent/insect control programs are undertaken by trained professionals. | | | | |
| 16. Items are stored in their original packing containers. | | | | |
| 17. Items that absorb odors are stored away from items that give off odors. | | | | |
| 18. All items are stored in covered containers. | | | | |
| 19. Personnel who maintain perpetual inventory records are not involved in taking follow-up physical inventory counts. | | | | |
| 20. When practical, items are issued only at specified times during the day. | | | | |

| Factor | Procedure | | Corrective Action | Requirements |
|---|---|---|---|---|
| | In Place | Not Done | | |
| 21. Personnel are trained to study recipes and to remove all required products from inventory areas at the same time. | | | | |
| 22. In small operations, food service management officials are physically present when items are withdrawn from inventory. | | | | |
| 23. Bin card systems are used in large operations to help provide special security for expensive items. | | | | |
| 24. Alcoholic beverages are issued on a bottle-for-bottle basis only (empty bottles are returned before full bottles are issued). | | | | |
| 25. Alcoholic beverages are issued to bars to replenish established bar levels. | | | | |
| 26. Trained accountants are in agreement about the method of inventory valuation which is in use. | | | | |
| 27. Inventory turnover levels are assessed monthly; trends (changes) in rates are carefully analyzed. | | | | |

| Factor | Procedure | | Corrective Action | Requirements |
|---|---|---|---|---|
| | In Place | Not Done | | |
| 28. Systems are in place to help assure that the optimal quantity of products in inventory is maintained. | | | | |
| 29. In large operations, completed issue requisitions are used as input to calculate daily food costs. | | | | |
| 30. Systems are in place to help assure that storage area temperature ranges are consistently within tolerable limits. | | | | |
| 31. A weekly report of items in storage longer than a specified time period is compiled; this information becomes input to food production plans. | | | | |

# 11. Product Preparation

| Factor | Procedure | | Corrective Action | Requirements |
|---|---|---|---|---|
| | In Place | Not Done | | |
| 1. Food production control procedures contribute to the need of the organization to supply products of the required quality. | | | | |
| 2. Standardized recipes are always used for the production of every product. | | | | |
| 3. Standard operating procedures define how products should be managed during time of production. | | | | |
| 4. All items produced in batches are tasted before being served. | | | | |
| 5. Employee training programs stress the requirement for products of a specified quality. | | | | |
| 6. Proper sanitation practices are always used when products are being prepared. | | | | |
| 7. Proper safety practices are always followed as items are being prepared. | | | | |

| Factor | Procedure | | Corrective Action | Requirements |
|---|---|---|---|---|
| | In Place | Not Done | | |
| 8. All tools/equipment required by all recipes are available and are in good repair. | | | | |
| 9. Preproduction planning is done to determine the quantity of items which should be produced. | | | | |
| 10. Tasks assigned to production personnel are written into employee schedules. | | | | |
| 11. Production supervisors are aware of critical time points which help to assure that work is completed on schedule. | | | | |
| 12. Sales history records are maintained for all products sold. | | | | |
| 13. Product sales history information is used to help assess expected income levels to be generated. | | | | |
| 14. A system is in place to match the amount of product issued with the quantity of product produced and sold. | | | | |
| 15. Procedures are in place to safely handle all leftovers. | | | | |

| Factor | Procedure | | Corrective Action | Requirements |
|---|---|---|---|---|
| | In Place | Not Done | | |
| 16. Menus are planned which consider both the preferences of the guests and the resources available to the operation. | | | | |
| 17. Only a reasonable amount of products judged necessary for production are issued to production centers. | | | | |
| 18. Procedures to minimize food waste are in place and are consistently used. | | | | |
| 19. Supervisors carefully monitor employee eating and drinking practices. | | | | |
| 20. Supervisors routinely study—and attempt to correct—production bottlenecks. | | | | |
| 21. All production equipment is carefully maintained to assure that it will remain in good working order. | | | | |
| 22. Systems to encourage effective communication between front- and back-of-house areas are in place. | | | | |

| Factor | Procedure | | Corrective Action | Requirements |
|---|---|---|---|---|
| | In Place | Not Done | | |
| 23. Studies are done to help assure that "convenience" foods are of proper quality and to effectively compensate for their higher food costs. | | | | |
| 24. Analyses are undertaken to help assure that labor saving equipment is cost-effective. | | | | |
| 25. Leftover reports are used to make future production decisions. | | | | |
| 26. All production personnel are always in required uniforms. | | | | |
| 27. All problems identified by internal and external sanitation/safety inspections are quickly addressed. | | | | |
| 28. A procedure to schedule production personnel according to a forecast of quantities of items to be produced is in place. | | | | |
| 29. In facilities with multi-food outlets, careful analysis is done to assess whether a commissary style production system should be used for selected items. | | | | |

| Factor | Procedure | | Corrective Action | Requirements |
|---|---|---|---|---|
| | In Place | Not Done | | |
| 30. Expensive items remaining in work station storage areas at the end of a shift are transferred back to central areas for more secure storage. | | | | |

# 12. Product Service

| Factor | Procedure | | Corrective Action | Requirements |
|---|---|---|---|---|
| | In Place | Not Done | | |
| 1. Food service personnel are neat in appearance; uniforms are clean. | | | | |
| 2. Food service personnel consistently follow proper hygiene procedures. | | | | |
| 3. Service ware is touched on handles (not on the eating surfaces). | | | | |
| 4. Clean food service towels are used to clean serving and eating surfaces. | | | | |
| 5. Food service staff has adequate menu knowledge (items available, preparation methods, and suggestions about appropriate items to accompany those being ordered). | | | | |
| 6. Food service personnel consistently practice proper courtesies and use appropriate etiquette. | | | | |
| 7. Service staff addresses guests by name when practical. | | | | |
| 8. Guests' (consumers') orders are taken promptly and properly. | | | | |

| Factor | Procedure | | Corrective Action | Requirements |
|---|---|---|---|---|
| | In Place | Not Done | | |
| 9. Service staff helps to assure that food served is appetizing; any problems are promptly reported to production personnel. | | | | |
| 10. Service personnel know and utilize appropriate suggestive selling techniques. | | | | |
| 11. Service staff consistently cooperates with all other employees both in production and service areas. | | | | |
| 12. Service personnel know how to properly utilize electronic data machines and other register equipment required to place orders. | | | | |
| 13. Service staff consistently "works clean." | | | | |
| 14. Service staff consistently complies with operating procedures designed to control sales income. | | | | |
| 15. Service personnel adequately perform appropriate beginning-and-end-of-shift side work requirements. | | | | |

| Factor | Procedure | | Corrective Action | Requirements |
|---|---|---|---|---|
| | In Place | Not Done | | |
| 16. Service staff consistently performs *mise-en-place* activities to help assure that there are adequate supplies of service ware and food items during each shift. | | | | |
| 17. Service personnel know and consistently use correct procedures for setting tables, serving food items and clearing tables. | | | | |
| 18. In table service properties, the following basic rules of table service are utilized:<br><br>a. Food is served from the guest's left with the server's left hand when appropriate; food is cleared from the guest's right with the server's right hand. | | | | |
| b. All beverages are served and removed from the guest's right with the server's right hand. | | | | |
| c. Soiled plates are not scraped in front of the guests. | | | | |
| d. Hot foods are always served hot; cold foods are always served cold. | | | | |

| Factor | Procedure | | Corrective Action | Requirements |
|---|---|---|---|---|
| | In Place | Not Done | | |
| e. Everyone in a party is normally served the same course simultaneously. | | | | |
| f. Water, coffee, and other applicable containers should be kept full; undesired glasses should promptly be removed. | | | | |
| g. Service personnel know the proper way to carry a loaded serving tray. | | | | |
| 19. In properties where counter service is utilized, the following principles are consistently followed:<br><br>a. Service personnel keep serving counters clean. | | | | |
| b. Foods which look unappetizing from lengthy steam table holding are not served. | | | | |
| c. Foods are replenished on a timely basis. | | | | |
| d. Food is garnished where practical on steam table pans to help make food attractive. | | | | |

| Factor | Procedure | | Corrective Action | Requirements |
|---|---|---|---|---|
| | In Place | Not Done | | |
| e. Foods are maintained at the proper temperature and all other sanitation precautions are consistently taken. | | | | |
| f. Proper portion control tools and techniques are consistently utilized. | | | | |
| g. When applicable, service personnel "empathize" with guests and serve the "best" portion remaining in the pan. | | | | |
| 20. Self-service salad, soup, potato or other bars are properly maintained to assure that they are both attractive and sanitary. | | | | |

# Part III | Labor Control Procedures

# 13. Employment and Personnel Management Practices*

| Factor | Yes | No |
|---|---|---|
| **Section 1:  Wage and Hour Laws**<br><br>1.  Record-keeping requirements: The following information is retained for all employees (some items may not be applicable if an employee is an exempt Executive, Administrative or Professional employee, or Outside Salesperson):<br><br>  a.  Employee's full name. | | |
|   b.  Address, including zip code. | | |
|   c.  Date of birth. | | |
|   d.  Sex. | | |
|   e.  Occupation in which employed. | | |
|   f.  Time and day of work when employee's workweek begins. | | |
|   g.  Hours worked each day. | | |
|   h.  Total hours worked each week. | | |
|   i.  Basis on which wages are paid (such as "6.50 per hour," "$250.00 a week," "Piecework"). | | |
|   j.  Regular hourly rate of pay for any week when overtime is worked. | | |
|   k.  Amount and nature of each payment excluded from the "regular rate." | | |
|   l.  Total daily or weekly straight-time earnings. | | |
|   m.  All additions or deductions from the employee's wages for each pay period. | | |

*From: Zaccarelli, H. and Ninemeier, J., *Cost Effective Contract Food Service: An Institutional Guide,* Second Edition (Winona, MN: Center for Business and Entrepreneurial Management, 1988), pp. 185–192.

| Factor | Yes | No |
|---|---|---|
| n. Total wages paid each pay period. | | |
| o. Dates of payment and the pay period covered by the payment. | | |
| 2. Are the above *complete* records kept for all employees? | | |
| 3. Are hours worked as accurately recorded as is reasonably possible? | | |
| 4. Are all records required by wage/hour regulations kept for at least three years? Are all records on which wage and hour computations are based kept for at least two years? | | |
| 5. Are all required posters current and posted? | | |
| 6. Personnel/Employment Actions. Are records retained of personnel or employment actions relating to the following items?<br><br>a. Job applications, resumes, or any other form of employment inquiry whenever submitted in response to an advertisement or other notice of existing or anticipated job openings, including records pertaining to the failure or refusal to hire any individual. | | |
| b. Promotion, demotion, transfer, selection for training, layoff, recall or discharge of any employee. | | |
| c. Job orders submitted to an employment agency or labor organization for recruitment of personnel for job openings. | | |
| d. Test papers completed by applicants or candidates for any position that disclose the results of any employer-administered aptitude or other employment test considered in connection with any personnel action. | | |
| e. The results of any physical examination where such examination is considered in connection with any personnel action. | | |
| f. Any advertisements or notices to the public or to employees relating to job openings, promotions, training programs, or opportunities for overtime work. | | |

| Factor | Yes | No |
|---|---|---|
| 7. If the above records are made, obtained or used, are they kept for one year from the date of the personnel action to which they relate (except in the case of applicants for temporary jobs)? | | |
| 8. Are application forms and other pre-employment records of applicants for temporary jobs kept for 90 days from the date of the personnel action? | | |
| 9. Are employee benefit plans and copies of seniority systems and merit systems that are in writing kept for the duration of the plan or system and for at least one year after its termination? | | |
| 10. Minimum wage.<br><br>   a. Do all employees on the payroll receive at least the applicable minimum wage? | | |
|    b. Does any company requirement that would cause expense to an employee (such as uniform requirements, tools furnished by employee, etc.) also ensure that the employee receives at least the minimum wage? | | |
|    c. Do any possible deductions made for uniforms, tools, etc., still leave employee's hourly wages at least the legal minimum? | | |
|    d. Does the company properly consider as employees all persons who are permitted to work (such as trainees, watchmen, maids, or janitors)? | | |
|    e. Does the company have any special certificates such as handicapped workers, learners, etc., which allow special minimum wage rates? If so, are the certificates current and are the terms of the certificate observed? | | |
|    f. Is all compensable waiting time, travel time, rest time, etc., being recorded and paid? | | |
|    g. Does the company make sure that no employees work "off the clock" (such as office workers answering the telephone during lunch, etc.)? | | |
|    h. Does all "pick-up" or "casual" labor receive at least the minimum wage? | | |
|    i. Are employees being paid for "break" time? | | |

| Factor | Yes | No |
|---|---|---|
| 11. Overtime. | | |
|    a. Do all hourly employees receive overtime after 40 hours per week? | | |
|    b. Do all employees that are on piecework or other forms of incentive pay receive overtime after 40 hours per week? | | |
|    c. Do all nonexempt salaried employees receive overtime after 40 hours per week? | | |
|    d. Are all exemptions from overtime currently claimed for employees valid? | | |
|    e. Is the overtime paid to employees at least time and one-half their actual earned or regular rate per hour? | | |
|    f. Are all appropriate "extras" included in the regular rate *before* computing overtime (such as shift differentials, incentive pay, etc.)? | | |
|    g. Are all bonuses that are not included in the regular pay properly excluded? | | |
|    h. Do all employees record their hours of work by punching a time clock or by some other method? | | |
|    i. Do all employees record their *actual* hours worked (as opposed to a *schedule* of hours)? | | |
|    j. Is a single workweek used as the standard when computing overtime? | | |
| 12. Child labor. | | |
|    a. Are all employees 18 years old or older? | | |
|    b. If "no": <br><br>     &bull; Is there proof of age on record for employees under 18 years old? | | |

| Factor | Yes | No |
|---|---|---|
| • Are all occupations that are included in the current Hazardous Occupations Orders performed only by employees who are 18 years or older? | | |
| • Are any employees 14 years old and over? | | |
| • Are any employees 16 years old and over? | | |
| • If under 16, do they work only between 7:00 A.M. and 7:00 P.M. in any one day, except during the summer (June 1 through Labor Day) when the evening hour is 9:00 P.M.? | | |
| • If under 16, do they work three hours or less per day when school is in session or eight hours or less a day when not in session? | | |
| • If under 16, do they work 18 hours or less per week when school is in session or 40 hours or less per week when not in session? | | |
| • Are 14- and 15-year-old minors employed only in the permitted occupations? | | |
| • Have all employees or agents of the company been instructed not to "hire" helpers on motor vehicles under 18 who could be considered employees of the company? | | |
| • Are all minors paid the applicable minimum wage? | | |
| • If not, are they employed at special minimum wages under the appropriate certificate? | | |
| • Do all minors receive proper overtime pay? | | |
| • Are current child labor permits maintained in the company's files for each minor? | | |
| • Are minors provided at least a 30-minute meal period at least once every 6 hours? | | |
| • Are male and female minors paid the same for equal work? | | |

| Factor | Yes | No |
|---|---|---|
| 13. Equal pay. (The Equal Pay Act applies only where substantially equal work is performed by both men and women. It does not apply to pay differentials that may exist among employees of one sex only, even though the employees involved may be performing substantially equal work.) If both male and female employees are employed in the establishment, check the questions below:<br><br>a. Are males and females who perform substantially equal work receiving the same rate of pay? | | |
| b. Are fringe benefits (for example, holiday pay, vacation pay, premium payments beyond statutory requirements) equal for male and female employees who do substantially equal work? | | |
| c. Where both men and women perform substantially equal work, are their wage rates the same even though the men may spend an insubstantial amount of time on duties that involve heavy lifting? | | |
| d. In comparing male and female jobs when pay is not equal, are the overall requirements as to skill, effort and responsibility considered in determining whether or not the jobs are equal? | | |
| e. If employees of one sex have been replaced by employees of the opposite sex on the same job, have the rates of pay and fringe benefits been the same? | | |
| f. Are actual job requirements and job performance used to determine whether men and women are performing substantially equal work rather than the job classification or "titles" of the men and women involved? | | |
| 14. Age discrimination.<br><br>a. Are help-wanted ads checked to see that they do not contain any preference, limitation, specification, or discrimination based on age? | | |
| b. Are job orders to employment agencies placed without any indications of age preference? | | |
| c. Do written or unwritten company policies provide for the employment of job applicants without limitation as to age? | | |

| Factor | Yes | No |
|---|---|---|
| d. Has the receptionist or have office employees been instructed never to discourage or turn away potential employees because of their age? | | |
| e. Has the organization kept a record of all employment inquiries submitted in response to its advertisements or other notices of job openings? | | |
| f. Are all employment applications (other than for temporary jobs) kept on file for a period of one year from the date of the personnel action? | | |
| g. Are newly hired employees in the 40 to 65 age group as well as under 40? | | |
| h. Are company employee promotions and discharges accomplished without age as a factor or consideration? | | |
| i. Do the company's policies provide the same benefits with respect to compensation, terms, conditions, or privileges of employment without regard to the individual employee's age? | | |
| **Section 2: Workmen's Compensation Laws**<br><br>1.  Coverage.<br><br>   a. Is the company covered by the law (usually three employees are required)? | | |
| b. Is the company exempt from the requirement of an insurance carrier (usually an exemption requires bonding or other evidence showing financial solvency)? | | |
| 2. Company records. Are records maintained pertaining to:<br><br>a. Number of employees? | | |
| b. Nature of their work? | | |
| c. Name of insurance company? | | |
| d. Number of policy? | | |

| Factor | Yes | No |
|---|---|---|
| e. Date of expiration of policy? | | |
| 3. Accident records.<br><br>a. For each accident, are the following records maintained?<br><br>• Name of injured or deceased employee? | | |
| • Address? | | |
| • Age? | | |
| • Wages? | | |
| • Time of accident? | | |
| • Cause of accident? | | |
| • Nature and extent of injury? | | |
| b. Are the proper state forms used to compile the above records? | | |
| c. If uninsured, has the company prepared a record of payments made? | | |
| d. Has the required poster been put up? | | |
| e. Is follow-up action taken to reduce the likelihood of a similar accident? | | |
| **Section 3: Unemployment Compensation Laws**<br><br>1. Company records. Do the company's employee records contain:<br><br>a. Name? | | |
| b. Social Security Number? | | |
| c. Dates of employment? | | |

| Factor | Yes | No |
|---|---|---|
| d. Gross earnings? | | |
| 2. Procedures. | | |
| a. Are the Unemployment Compensation "Request for Work Record" forms filled out completely and properly to ensure correct data in determining benefits? | | |
| b. Is the area on the form to dispute employee eligibility always completed, when appropriate, so that eligibility is not conceded? | | |
| c. Is a supporting statement always submitted when eligibility is challenged? | | |
| d. Does the supporting statement specify the time and place of the incident and the connection with the employee's employment? | | |
| e. When a violation of a company rule is involved, does the supporting statement contain:<br>• A quotation of the rule violated? | | |
| • An explanation of special circumstances supporting the reasonableness of the rule (if the rule is not self-explanatory or reasonable on its face)? | | |
| • A statement that the rule is well-established and is known to the employees? | | |
| • An explanation as to the extent to which the rule has been uniformly enforced? | | |
| f. Is a company representative and his or her telephone number designated to be contacted if Unemployment Compensation personnel need further information? | | |
| g. When claims are contested, is a company representative present at the fact-finding interview? | | |
| h. Are witnesses brought up at the hearing level? | | |

| Factor | Yes | No |
|---|---|---|
|    i. Are the Unemployment Compensation notices of claimants reviewed to spot errors in computations? | | |
|    j. Is any thought given to offer a claimant other employment so that he can reject it and possibly terminate his benefits? | | |
|    k. Is a labor dispute that interrupts work promptly reported to the Job Service Office? | | |
|    l. Does the report contain: | | |
|      &bull; The date the dispute began? | | |
|      &bull; The nature of the dispute? | | |
|      &bull; The establishment involved? | | |
|      &bull; The number of employees employed before the dispute? | | |
|      &bull; The number of employees out of work because of the dispute? | | |
| 3. Posters. Are appropriate notices posted and accessible to employees, as required by law? | | |
| **Section 4: Discipline and Grievance Activities** | | |
| 1. Are the facts of a disciplinary offense properly investigated: | | |
|    a. Do employees have an opportunity to tell their side of the story? | | |
|    b. Do the immediate supervisors check for verification of the stories? | | |
|    c. Are all sources of information investigated? | | |
|    d. Is discrimination shown toward any individual or group? | | |

| Factor | Yes | No |
|---|---|---|
| 2. Are corrective measures administered properly: | | |
|    a. Are considerations made as to whether individual or collective aciton be taken? | | |
|    b. Are explanations given to the employee as to why action is taken? | | |
|    c. Are explanations given as to how to prevent similar offenses in the future and warnings administered? | | |
|    d. Are memoranda for the record prepared for all disciplinary actions, copies given to the employees, and opportunities afforded for rebuttal? | | |
|    e. In determining a penalty, is the seriousness of the employee's conduct considered in relation to his or her particular job and employment record? | | |
|    f. Is discipline treated as a corrective measure (not as a reprisal for an offense)? | | |
| 3. Has there been the necessary follow-up: | | |
|    a. Have the measures taken had the desired effect? Is this monitored? | | |
|    b. Have steps been taken to overcome any resentment? | | |
|    c. Have the measures had the desired effect on other employees in the department? Is this monitored? | | |
| 4. If a union contract is involved, have the contract provisions been adhered to: | | |
|    a. Have grievances been reduced to proper written form? | | |
|    b. Have all the steps been followed? | | |
|    c. Have answers been filed in a timely way? | | |

| Factor | Yes | No |
|---|---|---|
| d. Have the grievants and/or their representatives been present when required? | | |
| e. Have the negotiations or discussions properley distilled the issues? | | |
| f. Have demands for arbitration been properly and promptly presented? | | |
| **Section 5: Basic Supervision Practices** | | |
| 1. Security needs. | | |
| a. Is there a complaint or grievance procedure? | | |
| b. Does management listen to employee gripes? | | |
| c. Does management follow up and investigate gripes? | | |
| d. Are seniority principles observed? | | |
| e. Are warnings given before disciplinary action or discharge? | | |
| 2. Employee expectation needs. | | |
| a. Is periodic appraisal of performances made by supervisors? | | |
| b. Are company rules and regulations unified? | | |
| c. Are company rules and regulations known and communicated? | | |
| d. Do company rules and regulations impose unfair standards? | | |
| e. Is adequate training given for each job? | | |
| 3. Employee participation needs. | | |
| a. Are employees' suggestions given consideration? | | |

| Factor | Yes | No |
|---|---|---|
| b. Are job changes made without the employee being informed? | | |
| c. Are job changes made without consultation with the employee? | | |
| d. Are there channels of communication between employees and management? | | |
| 4. Working condition needs.<br><br>a. Is there proper ventilation? | | |
| b. Are there good rest and employee dining areas? | | |
| c. Is there good and adequate parking? | | |
| d. Are the restrooms clean? | | |
| e. Is there proper lighting, temperature, clean work areas, and an absence of safety hazards? | | |
| 5. Employee information needs.<br><br>a. Are employees informed about wage scales? | | |
| b. Are employees informed about company benefits and what they mean? | | |
| c. Are employees informed about expansion, new management, new supervisors, and promotions? | | |
| d. Are employees informed about new methods and equipment? | | |
| e. Are employees informed about company plans, profits, sales, etc.? | | |
| 6. Advancement/promotion needs.<br><br>a. Are promotions made from within? | | |

| Factor | Yes | No |
|---|---|---|
| b. Is consideration given to employees? | | |
| c. Do employees know how to work for promotion? | | |
| d. Do employees know why promotions have not been made? | | |
| e. Are employees informed of promotions from within? | | |
| 7. Adequate compensation needs.<br><br>a. Are wages competitive with like jobs in other companies in the same industry and the same operating area? | | |
| b. Are increases made either on a general or merit basis? | | |
| c. Are employees informed about wage scales and how to make increases? | | |
| d. Is there favoritism, i.e., different employees receiving different rates for the same job? | | |
| 8. Employee benefit needs.<br><br>a. Are benefits competitive with other companies in the same industry and the same operating area? | | |
| b. Do the benefits meet the basic needs of the employees? | | |
| c. Are benefits paid to food service employees similar to those paid to non-dietary staff? | | |
| 9. Personnel policies.<br><br>a. Are personnel policies written? | | |
| b. Are personnel policies published and communicated? | | |
| c. Are personnel policies understood? | | |

| Factor | Yes | No |
|---|---|---|
| d. Do personnel policies meet the needs of management and employees? | | |
| e. Is there favoritism in application of policies? | | |
| f. Are promises broken? | | |
| 10. Identification needs. <br><br> a. Do employees have a sense of belonging? | | |
| b. Are employees treated as individuals? | | |
| c. Does management run company *with* employees? | | |
| d. Do employees participate in change? | | |
| **Section 6: Basic Personnel Administration Practices** <br><br> 1. Do the job descriptions available accurately reflect all tasks perfomed by all positions in all sections within the food service department? Are they revised as necessary? | | |
| 2. Are personnel aware of tasks in the job descriptions; do job descriptions effectively set boundaries of responsibility for each position? | | |
| 3. Are job specifications available and used in employee selection to ensure that personnel with proper qualifications are hired? | | |
| 4. Is an organization chart used, and revised as necessary, to show relationships between and among sections and positions within the food service department? | | |
| 5. Are new employees given copies of job descriptions, specifications, and an organization chart, along with materials in an employee handbook, at the time of hiring? | | |
| 6. Are supervisors involved in (interview applicants for and participate in making a decision about) hiring for vacant positions in their section? | | |

| Factor | Yes | No |
|---|---|---|
| 7. When possible, are current eligible employees promoted to fill vacant positions; is there a "career ladder" of planned progression for employees in the food service department (for example, food service worker to assistant head cook to cook)? | | |
| 8. Are supervisors aware of and do they work with informal employee groups in the food service department? | | |
| 9. Are only qualified applicants considered for vacant positions? | | |
| 10. Is an employee application form used as the initial step in the selection process? | | |
| 11. Are references on employee application forms asked about applicants? | | |
| 12. Is an interview between the food service director or other food service officials and the applicant held before the selection is finalized? | | |
| 13. Is an interview between the supervisor/section head and the applicant held before the selection is finalized? | | |
| 14. Do top food service officials and the section supervisor discuss and make a joint decision regarding the applicant? | | |
| 15. Are simple tests (such as extending a recipe or working the dish machine) used to ensure that "experienced" personnel can be further trained? | | |
| 16. Are several applicants considered for each position; is the best selected? | | |
| 17. Is the selection process designed so that the applicant can learn about the property (in addition to food service personnel learning about the applicant)? | | |
| 18. Is a new employee given a tour of the property and introduced to all possible people *before* being taken to the work station? | | |
| 19. Is the formal work group notified in advance of the new employee's arrival; are his or her job qualifications explained? | | |

| Factor | Yes | No |
|---|---|---|
| 20. Does the supervisor spend some time with the new employee on the first day to make him or her feel comfortable and to answer basic questions? | | |
| 21. Is an experienced employee assigned to the new employee to "help out" with other questions and to begin required on-the-job training? | | |
| 22. Is a planned training program undertaken to ensure that the new employee, even if experienced, is able to perform required tasks according to required procedures? | | |
| 23. Do the trainer and supervisor formally discuss needs, if any, for additional training and evaluate the new employee's progress in the learner of job tasks? | | |
| 24. Is training used to improve (bring up to minimum quality standards) the performance of long-time employees who are not working according to required procedures? | | |
| 25. Is a formal employee evaluation program used to enable supervisors to inform employees about strengths and weaknesses and to permit employees to talk with supervisors about ways they (employees) feel that their jobs can be improved? | | |
| 26. Do employees know, in advance, the job standards on which they will be evaluated and are they then given training to permit them to achieve these standards? | | |
| **Section 7: Basic Procedures in a Labor Cost Control System** | | |
| 1. Has a labor hours staffing guide been developed to help supervisors schedule variable labor employees? | | |
| 2. Are salaried personnel scheduled according to need (salaried labor is *not* generally used to replace hourly paid employees)? Are tasks performed by salaried personnel commensurate with salaries being paid? | | |
| 3. Do the supervisors and the food service director know, for each position in the section, the number of labor hours needed to perform work to minimum quality levels (for varied sales volumes if there is a fluctuating patient census)? | | |

| Factor | Yes | No |
|---|---|---|
| 4. Do the section supervisor and/or other food service officials regularly observe work performed by personnel in all positions to ensure that the staffing guide accurately reflects the necessary number of labor hours needed? | | |
| 5. Are staffing guides developed separately for each shift if type of menu, variety of items served, etc., are judged to affect worker productivity rates? | | |
| 6. Do supervisors use the Variable Labor Staffing guide when scheduling employees; are only the maximum number of labor hours judged necessary scheduled for each shift? | | |
| 7. Do supervisors make more use of split shifts, part-time personnel, and staggered scheduling to ensure that personnel are available *only* when needed? | | |
| 8. Are employees informed about their work schedule through use of a formal schedule posted in an employee area? Are schedules made at least one week in advance? | | |
| 9. Do supervisors confirm the number of labor hours worked by variable cost employees? Is a report signed by each supervisor, indicating for each employee the number of labor hours worked, included as an integral part of the facility's payroll system? | | |
| 10. Are supervisors required to explain why the actual number of labor hours worked by employees within a position exceeded the standard (planned) number of labor hours? | | |
| 11. Does the food service director carefully review all weekly reports to note trends and to take corrective action when actual labor hours within a section consistently (frequently) exceed standard (planned) labor hours? | | |
| 12. Are the reasons for excessive labor hours known and is necessary corrective action taken? | | |
| 13. Do the food service director, perhaps other food service officials, and the supervisor work together in planning for and monitoring results of corrective actions taken to control labor costs? | | |
| 14. Is a standard labor hour cost control system used to monitor/control labor costs? Are systems involving labor cost dollars and budget development and use considered for their applicability to the individual property's needs? | | |

| Factor | Yes | No |
|---|---|---|
| **Section 8: Basic Personnel Supervision Practices**<br><br>1. Do all supervisors recognize that employee motivation and training tasks are part of their jobs? | | |
| 2. Do all supervisors recognize that most employee problems are manageable and that they frequently result from use of improper supervisory techniques? | | |
| 3. Do supervisors know how to give instructions properly; do they seek cooperation and, when necessary, take time to explain, defend, and justify reasons for actions to be taken? | | |
| 4. Have supervisors been taught procedures of motivation and direction? | | |
| 5. Are supervisors aware of procedures that can be used to change employee attitudes? | | |
| 6. Are supervisors aware of and do they attempt to provide those things that employees desire from their jobs? | | |
| 7. Are supervisors aware of facts that affect employee morale levels and do they constantly work to improve morale? | | |
| 8. Are supervisors able to make good use of the decision-making/problem-solving process to get their jobs done as effectively as possible? | | |
| 9. Do supervisors obtain ideas from all affected parties when decisions are to be made? | | |
| 10. Are supervisors aware of and do they know how to work with special types of employees (those who are careless, old, young, handicapped, etc.)? | | |
| 11. Are supervisors and the food service director aware that, in some instances, the supervisor is "part of the problem"? (Changes must sometimes be made by the supervisor as well as by the employees.) | | |
| 12. Are supervisors fair and reasonable as they discipline employees; is discipline designed to create adherence to fair and reasonable procedures rather than to punish for wrongdoing? | | |

| Factor | Yes | No |
|---|---|---|
| 13. Do supervisors help make decisions regarding promotion of their staff? | | |
| 14. Are supervisors involved in decisions regarding employee termination? | | |
| **Section 9: Basic Work Simplification Practices**<br><br>1. Do supervisors know how to analyze jobs with the intent of improving the work being performed? | | |
| 2. Is the philosophy of work simpification an integral, ongoing part of the supervisor's job? | | |
| 3. Do supervisors undertake a constant process of reviewing work with the intent to eliminate, simplify, or combine tasks being performed? | | |
| 4. Are supervisors aware of "signs" that indicate an examination of work tasks is in order? | | |
| 5. Do supervisors know procedures that should be used to analyze a job for work simpification improvements? | | |
| 6. Can supervisors recognize problems, and do they know how to correct them as jobs are being examined? | | |
| 7. Do supervisors encourage employees to help with work simplification; do they inform employees that work improvement is to their (employees') advantage? | | |

# 14. Management of Staff

| Factor | In Practice (✓) | | | If "No" (✓) | | | | |
|---|---|---|---|---|---|---|---|---|
| | Yes | No | Not Applicable | Policy Needed | Procedure Needed | Training Needed | Responsible Person | Compliance Date |
| 1. Common causes of personnel irritation are known and addressed. | | | | | | | | |
| 2. There is a planned "career ladder" and professional progam for interested staff members in place. | | | | | | | | |
| 3. A detailed orientation program for new employees is utilized. | | | | | | | | |
| 4. Job descriptions accurately reflect all tasks performed by those in all positions. | | | | | | | | |
| 5. Personnel are aware of tasks in the job descriptions. | | | | | | | | |
| 6. Job specifications are available and used in employee selection to ensure that personnel with proper qualifications are hired. | | | | | | | | |
| 7. An organization chart is used, and revised as necessary, to show relationships between and among sections and positions within each department. | | | | | | | | |

| Factor | In Practice (√) | | | If "No" (√) | | | | |
|---|---|---|---|---|---|---|---|---|
| | Yes | No | Not Applicable | Policy Needed | Procedure Needed | Training Needed | Responsible Person | Compliance Date |
| 8. New employees are given copies of job descriptions, specifications, and an organization chart, along with materials in an employee handbook at the time of hiring. | | | | | | | | |
| 9. Supervisors are involved in (interview applicants for and participate in making a decision about) hiring for vacant positions. | | | | | | | | |
| 10. When possible, currently employed, eligible employees are promoted to fill vacant positions. | | | | | | | | |
| 11. Supervisors are aware of and work with informal employee groups. | | | | | | | | |
| 12. Only qualified applicants are considered for positions. | | | | | | | | |
| 13. Training is used to improve the performance of long-time employees who are not working according to required procedures. | | | | | | | | |
| 14. A formal employee evaluation program is used to enable supervisors to inform employees about strengths and weaknesses. | | | | | | | | |

| Factor | In Practice (✓) | | | If "No" (✓) | | | | |
|---|---|---|---|---|---|---|---|---|
| | Yes | No | Not Applicable | Policy Needed | Procedure Needed | Training Needed | Responsible Person | Compliance Date |
| 15. Employees know, in advance, about the job standards on which they will be evaluated. | | | | | | | | |
| 16. A labor hours staffing guide has been developed to help supervisors schedule variable labor employees. | | | | | | | | |
| 17. Salaried personnel are scheduled according to need (salaried labor is *not* generally used to replace hourly paid employees). | | | | | | | | |
| 18. Employees are informed about their work schedule through use of a formal schedule posted in an employee area. | | | | | | | | |
| 19. Supervisors confirm the number of labor hours worked by variable cost employees. | | | | | | | | |
| 20. The manager carefully reviews all weekly reports to note trends and to take corrective action when actual labor hours within a section consistently exceed standard labor hours. | | | | | | | | |
| 21. The reasons for excessive labor are known. | | | | | | | | |

# Part IV | Other Resource Control Procedures

## 15. Personal Time Management Procedures

| Factor | I Do This | | If I Want to Do This | | Comments |
|---|---|---|---|---|---|
| | Yes | No | What Must I Do First? | When Will I Begin? | |
| 1. I develop and use a daily time plan which specifies priority activities. | | | | | |
| 2. I try to limit telephone calls (incoming and outgoing) to specific time periods. | | | | | |
| 3. I set—and keep—appointments with sales representatives. | | | | | |
| 4. I have—and maintain—specific agendas and time schedules for meetings. | | | | | |
| 5. I keep my desk and files (manual and electronic) organized. | | | | | |
| 6. I delegate all possible activities to subordinates (even those "I've always done" and those I like to do). | | | | | |
| 7. I use my experience to help establish and judge allowable times for specified projects. | | | | | |
| 8. I have set up clear lines of responsibility and authority (the organization chart is current!). | | | | | |

| Factor | I Do This | | If I Want to Do This | | Comments |
|---|---|---|---|---|---|
| | **Yes** | **No** | **What Must I Do First?** | **When Will I Begin?** | |
| 9. I pass all necessary information "down the organization" on a timely basis. | | | | | |
| 10. I procrastinate only as a decisive management strategy—not as part of a *laissez-faire* management style. | | | | | |
| 11. Procedures incorporate standards of expectation and status reports so I can monitor progress. | | | | | |
| 12. I allow time for my own professional and personal development. | | | | | |
| 13. I allow time for adequate rest and exercise. | | | | | |
| 14. I know how my time is currently spent. | | | | | |
| 15. I know how to minimize interruptions. | | | | | |
| 16. I know how to break big projects into small parts and schedule time for the small elements. | | | | | |
| 17. I know how to delegate (see Checklist 30 in Part V, page 125). | | | | | |

84

| Factor | I Do This | | If I Want to Do This | | Comments |
|---|---|---|---|---|---|
| | Yes | No | What Must I Do First? | When Will I Begin? | |
| 18. I get angry with myself when I do not adhere to self-imposed time schedules. | | | | | |
| 19. I spend time on what I *have* to do rather than on what I *like* to do. | | | | | |
| 20. I effectively manage time spent in group meetings. | | | | | |
| 21. I analyze and correct procedures leading to mistakes so time does not need to be wasted in redundant work. | | | | | |
| 22. I combine similar tasks (such as making phone calls) and do them at the same time. | | | | | |
| 23. I have developed and use work simplification procedures to make my work easier. | | | | | |

# 16. Management of Equipment

| Factor | In Practice (✓) | | | If "No" (✓) | | | | |
|---|---|---|---|---|---|---|---|---|
| | Yes | No | Not Applicable | Policy Needed | Procedure Needed | Training Needed | Responsible Person | Compliance Date |
| 1. Equipment purchases are justified by acceptable cost/benefit, payback, and/or other analyses. | | | | | | | | |
| 2. All applicable equipment is maintained under an appropriate preventive maintenance program. | | | | | | | | |
| 3. Personnel knowledgeable and trained in proper maintenance/repair procedures are available as needed. | | | | | | | | |
| 4. Performance/repair records are kept for all major equipment items. | | | | | | | | |
| 5. Tax accountants are involved as necessary in decisions involving equipment purchases (cash, installment purchase, leasing and/or other acquisition options). | | | | | | | | |
| 6. Analyses are routinely undertaken to assure that labor-savings advantages of equipment are incorporated into work procedures. | | | | | | | | |
| 7. Employees are trained to operate equipment correctly and safely. | | | | | | | | |

| Factor | In Practice (✓) | | | If "No" (✓) | | | | |
|---|---|---|---|---|---|---|---|---|
| | Yes | No | Not Applicable | Policy Needed | Procedure Needed | Training Needed | Responsible Person | Compliance Date |
| 8. Responsibilities of buyer and seller for installation of equipment are understood before the first equipment purchase decision is made. | | | | | | | | |
| 9. Optional equipment features are objectively analyzed before purchase commitments are made. | | | | | | | | |
| 10. All new equipment is compatible (when necessary) with existing equipment. | | | | | | | | |

# 17. Management of Money

| Factor | In Practice (✓) | | | If "No" (✓) | | | | |
|---|---|---|---|---|---|---|---|---|
| | Yes | No | Not Applicable | Policy Needed | Procedure Needed | Training Needed | Responsible Person | Compliance Date |
| 1. An operating budget is used as a profit plan and to monitor the facility's ongoing financial performance. | | | | | | | | |
| 2. Profit goals for addressing return on investment or return on asset requirements have been established. | | | | | | | | |
| 3. Accountants are used as advisors—not as decision-makers. | | | | | | | | |
| 4. Adequate security controls to safeguard cash sales before deposit are in place. | | | | | | | | |
| 5. Adequate back office security controls are utilized to protect cash during times of bank deposit, account verification, and accounts receivable and payable. | | | | | | | | |
| 6. Budget reforecasting systems are in use to update this important control tool. | | | | | | | | |
| 7. Allowable levels of variance between planned and actual operating results are established; corrective actions are taken when these levels are exceeded. | | | | | | | | |

| Factor | In Practice (✓) | | | If "No" (✓) | | | | |
| --- | --- | --- | --- | --- | --- | --- | --- | --- |
| | Yes | No | Not Applicable | Policy Needed | Procedure Needed | Training Needed | Responsible Person | Compliance Date |
| 8. Advice is sought from tax accountants as inventory valuation methods and/or equipment depreciation systems are determined. | | | | | | | | |
| 9. Basic principles of managerial accounting are understood and utilized. | | | | | | | | |

# 18. Management of Personal Work Methods

| Factor | In Practice (✓) | | | If "No" (✓) | | | | |
|---|---|---|---|---|---|---|---|---|
| | Yes | No | Not Applicable | Policy Needed | Procedure Needed | Training Needed | Responsible Person | Compliance Date |
| 1. I constantly question work procedures being used to assure that the best procedures are in use. | | | | | | | | |
| 2. I delegate in order to do the work I should do—not that I want to do. | | | | | | | | |
| 3. I use time management principles to work on the most important things first. | | | | | | | | |
| 4. I know what equipment will—and will not—do. | | | | | | | | |
| 5. I am aware of the ever increasing number of computer applications available to make my work easier. | | | | | | | | |
| 6. I don't "reinvent the wheel"; when I'm trying something new I ask others—including subordinates—for ideas. | | | | | | | | |
| 7. I keep on learning; the old saying "there's always a better way" is often true. | | | | | | | | |

| Factor | In Practice (✓) | | | If "No" (✓) | | | | |
|---|---|---|---|---|---|---|---|---|
| | Yes | No | Not Applicable | Policy Needed | Procedure Needed | Training Needed | Responsible Person | Compliance Date |
| 8. I make sure that job descriptions are current and accurate—and that staff members are performing the work they should be doing. | | | | | | | | |
| 9. I know how work should be done—and train and supervise my staff to assure that this is how work is done. | | | | | | | | |
| 10. I maximize available human resources and, when practical, use participative management techniques. | | | | | | | | |
| 11. I try to solve problems affecting work rather than resign myself to them. | | | | | | | | |
| 12. I recognize my limitations and make the best of the situation. | | | | | | | | |

91

# Part V | Other Supervision Activities

## 19. Personal Decision-Making Principles

| Factor | Factor Utilized | | Training Strategy, If Any, to Be Used |
|---|---|---|---|
| | Yes | No | |
| 1. I utilize a basic, common-sense approach to decision-making, which involves: | | | |
| a. Definition of the problem. | | | |
| b. Generation of practical alternatives. | | | |
| c. Evaluation of alternatives. | | | |
| d. Selection of alternative. | | | |
| e. Trial implementation of chosen alternative. | | | |
| f. Evaluation of trial study. | | | |
| g. Implementation of revised alternative. | | | |
| 2. When necessary, I seek a "satisfactory" rather than "ideal" outcome to my decisions. | | | |
| 3. I delegate simple, "programmed" decisions to others. | | | |
| 4. I use group participative approaches, when practical, to generate alternatives for decisions to be made. | | | |
| 5. I allow employees who will be affected by decisions to provide input to the decision-making process when possible. | | | |

95

| Factor | Factor Utilized | | Training Strategy, If Any, to Be Used |
| --- | --- | --- | --- |
| | Yes | No | |
| 6. I generally have or can obtain all required information necessary to make a decision. | | | |
| 7. I evaluate alternative solutions in terms of organizational goals and their perceived impact upon problem resolution. | | | |
| 8. I consider implementation issues as resolution alternatives are evaluated. | | | |
| 9. I recognize that affected employees may resist changes required by decisions (see Checklist 22, Part V, page 102). | | | |
| 10. I regularly evaluate decisions which are made on an as-needed basis (but, generally, consider both short- and long-term implications). | | | |
| 11. I use experience to supplement my common sense and written information when making decisions. | | | |
| 12. When practical, my decisions yield practical alternatives; they are flexible. | | | |

# 20. Conflict Management Principles

| Factor | Factor Utilized | | Training Strategy, If Any, to Be Used |
|---|---|---|---|
| | Yes | No | |
| 1. Some conflict is inevitable and even necessary to attain some goals of the food service department. | | | |
| 2. Some conflict does—and some does not—harm people and hinder attainment of food service department goals. | | | |
| 3. Intergroup competition occurs when: | | | |
| a. There is a need to share resources. | | | |
| b. There is a different perception of goals. | | | |
| c. Work activities are dependent upon each other. | | | |
| d. There are different perceptions in values or goals. | | | |
| 4. There are times when conflict can be helpful (for example, it can stimulate groups to find better solutions to problems). | | | |
| 5. Conflict can be stimulated by: | | | |
| a. Bringing in outsiders. | | | |
| b. Restructuring the organization. | | | |
| c. Encouraging competition. | | | |

| Factor | Factor Utilized | | Training Strategy, If Any, to Be Used |
|---|---|---|---|
| | Yes | No | |
| d. Selecting the "right" manager for differing work groups. | | | |
| 6. Some examples of methods of reducing conflict are: | | | |
| a. Establishment of mutually acceptable goals. | | | |
| b. Efforts to unite the group against a common "threat." | | | |
| 7. Conflict can be suppressed by: | | | |
| a. Force (power). | | | |
| b. Diplomacy. | | | |
| c. Avoidance. | | | |
| d. Majority rule. | | | |
| 8. One can resolve conflict through compromise actions. | | | |
| 9. Joint problem-solving between groups can be used to resolve conflict. | | | |
| 10. Line/staff conflicts can be reduced by: | | | |
| a. Clearly indicating responsibilities. | | | |

| Factor | Factor Utilized | | Training Strategy, If Any, to Be Used |
| --- | --- | --- | --- |
| | Yes | No | |
| b. Increasing staff/line consultations. | | | |
| c. Teaching line employees how to properly utilize staff personnel. | | | |
| d. Holding both line and staff employees accountable for predetermined results. | | | |

# 21. Managing Informal Groups

| Factor | Factor Utilized | | Training Strategy, If Any, to Be Used |
|---|---|---|---|
| | Yes | No | |
| 1. Managers must be concerned about and recognize informal work groups. | | | |
| 2. Employees who have no type of social contact at work often find their job unsatisfying. | | | |
| 3. Informal groups provide many benefits for their members. | | | |
| 4. Success of informal groups depends upon their internal strength. | | | |
| 5. Managers must try to influence informal groups to accept desires of the food service department. | | | |
| 6. Managers should try to keep formal activities from unnecessarily threatening informal groups. | | | |
| 7. Managers should involve informal group members in plans and, when possible, try to mesh the goals of formal and informal groups. | | | |
| 8. Group decision-making is important when mistakes must be avoided and when ample time for group deliberations is available. | | | |
| 9. Group pressure often influences an employee's reaction to a management directive. | | | |

| Factor | Factor Utilized | | Training Strategy, If Any, to Be Used |
| --- | --- | --- | --- |
| | Yes | No | |
| 10. Eliminating management actions designed to harm informal groups can foster groups which will be beneficial to the food service department. | | | |
| 11. The informal grapevine can be effectively used to distribute information. | | | |
| 12. Organizing and directing activities are easier when informal groups cooperate with the food service manager. | | | |
| 13. The "sum" of group efforts is usually more than the singular activities of each group member. | | | |
| 14. Food service supervisors can be influential in helping employees join informal work groups which are helpful to the department. | | | |
| 15. Generally, between-group competition within the food service department causes more harm than it creates positive benefits. | | | |
| 16. Food service supervisors are generally incorrect when they force employees to choose between the informal group and the supervisor. | | | |
| 17. Employees are affected by "outside" forces other than informal groups as they attempt to perform their jobs. | | | |

# 22. Managing Change

| Factor | Factor Utilized | | Training Strategy, If Any, to Be Used |
|---|---|---|---|
| | Yes | No | |
| 1. When change is needed, either people or the situation (or both) must be changed. | | | |
| 2. People-approaches to change attempt to change attitudes. | | | |
| 3. Organizational approaches to change focus on change within the environment which will "automatically" require people to change behavior. | | | |
| 4. In order to change people, there must first be dissatisfaction with present conditions. | | | |
| 5. Changes are easier to implement when: | | | |
| a. There is lessened support for old attitudes. | | | |
| b. The work place is filled with positive implications of the change. | | | |
| c. There is reinforcement of actions favoring change. | | | |
| 6. Training and education programs can be helpful in implementing change. | | | |
| 7. There is a basic human tendency to resist change and to retain the status quo. | | | |

| Factor | Factor Utilized | | Training Strategy, If Any, to Be Used |
| --- | --- | --- | --- |
| | Yes | No | |
| 8. Change can best be brought about when the need for change is explained and defended. | | | |
| 9. Input in the process leading to change by those affected by the change can be very helpful in implementing changes. | | | |
| 10. A process of systematic change can be used to implement necessary changes. | | | |
| 11. Conditions which must be present for change to be effectively incorporated include openness, honesty, mutual respect, courage and commitment. | | | |

103

# 23. Managing Employee Discipline

| Factor | Factor Utilized | | Training Strategy, If Any, to Be Used |
|---|---|---|---|
| | Yes | No | |
| 1. Proper discipline can be administered only when specifics of each situation and when the employee's background and work record are known. | | | |
| 2. The authority of a supervisor's disciplinary ability should be specified in his/her job description. | | | |
| 3. Precedents covering similar situations should be known; there is a need for consistency in the treatment of employees. | | | |
| 4. Special situations involved in employee misconduct should be considered. | | | |
| 5. Punishment should match the offense. | | | |
| 6. Punishment should become progressively more severe when the same employee problem(s) continue(s). | | | |
| 7. The employee's side of the situation should be known. | | | |
| 8. Disciplining should be done in private. | | | |
| 9. Supervisors should not act in anger. | | | |
| 10. Being lenient does not always correlate with "being liked." | | | |
| 11. Supervisors should never discipline for vindictive (revengeful) reasons. | | | |

| Factor | Factor Utilized | | Training Strategy, If Any, to Be Used |
|---|---|---|---|
| | Yes | No | |
| 12. Supervisors should never delegate their responsibility to discipline to some other person or department. | | | |
| 13. Records of discipline activities should be maintained. | | | |
| 14. Self-discipline is the best discipline. | | | |
| 15. The discipline process should begin as soon as possible after a policy or rule violation is discovered. | | | |
| 16. Employees must know in advance what is expected of them. | | | |
| 17. Employee handbooks are often good sources of policies upon which discipline activities may be directed. | | | |
| 18. It should be possible (even in a non-union operation) for an employee to appeal a disciplinary action to higher level(s) of management. | | | |

## 24. Management by Objectives (MBO)

| Factor | Factor Utilized | | Training Strategy, If Any, to Be Used |
|--------|------|-----|------|
| | Yes | No | |
| 1. All managers must have clearly defined objectives that specifically apply to their function. | | | |
| 2. The objectives of each manager must relate to organizational goals. | | | |
| 3. Managers at each level should contribute to higher level objectives. | | | |
| 4. Each manager should contribute to the development of his/her own goals. | | | |
| 5. Each manager must perform a self-appraisal of the extent to which goals were attained. | | | |
| 6. Each manager must review the status of objective attainment with his/her supervisor; objectives are then mutually developed for the next period. | | | |
| 7. All objectives should be stated in objective, easy-to-measure format. | | | |
| 8. A manager must be given discretion in selecting ways to attain established objectives. | | | |
| 9. Discussion about and plans to resolve problems should be part of sessions held to review attainment of objectives. | | | |
| 10. To be effective, MBO programs must be continually supported by management at all organizational levels. | | | |

106

| Factor | Factor Utilized | | Training Strategy, If Any, to Be Used |
| --- | --- | --- | --- |
| | Yes | No | |
| 11. Managers who successfully attain MBO goals generally set new goals with higher levels of performance. | | | |
| 12. Performance will improve when goals are realistic and when goals are accepted by the affected staff. | | | |
| 13. Providing employees with feedback about their performance will help to further improve performance. | | | |
| 14. MBO programs have individual employee as well as organizational advantages; individuals know what is expected of them and know the bases upon which they will be evaluated. | | | |
| 15. Problems which hinder goal attainment in one period should be considered as goals for future periods. | | | |
| 16. MBO objectives which are written should avoid dual accountability; a person's objectives should only relate to areas for which he/she is accountable. | | | |
| 17. MBO cannot be implemented when a structured and inflexible program of staff management is utilized. | | | |

# 25. Performance Appraisal

| Factor | Now Done | Review Needed | Not Relevant | Comments |
|---|---|---|---|---|
| 1. Factors in appraisal reviews focus on performance—not on personal traits (characteristics). | | | | |
| 2. The purpose of performance appraisal includes identifying problems so corrective action can be taken; the purpose is not just to find fault with past performance. | | | | |
| 3. The performance appraisal focuses on tasks defined by the job description. | | | | |
| 4. Effective forms are used for performance review purposes; they permit expected and actual results to be quantified. | | | | |
| 5. Performance reviews are held on a regularly scheduled basis. | | | | |
| 6. Supervisors are trained in skills required to conduct effective performance appraisals. | | | | |
| 7. The performance appraisal process is kept as simple as possible. | | | | |
| 8. Performance reviews center on comparing employee performance to required performance—not on comparing one employee against another. | | | | |
| 9. Follow-up actions identified as part of the performance review process are undertaken and monitored. | | | | |

| Factor | Now Done | Review Needed | Not Relevant | Comments |
|---|---|---|---|---|
| 10. When applicable, employees have input to decisions about the mechanics used to conduct performance reviews. | | | | |
| 11. Supervisors consider the conduct of performance reviews to be an important and integral part of their job. | | | | |
| 12. Employees are aware of all objectives of performance evaluation. | | | | |
| 13. Employee reaction to discussions held by the supervisor is encouraged. | | | | |
| 14. Appeal procedures for employee evaluations have been established. | | | | |
| 15. Supervisors are trained in effective interview techniques which should be used for the appraisal process. | | | | |
| 16. Employees are asked what supervisors can do—or should not do—to help them in their improvement efforts. | | | | |
| 17. Interim performance reviews are used as necessary between dates scheduled for formal appraisals. | | | | |
| 18. Effective two-way communication is used during the appraisal process. | | | | |
| 19. Facts are available to support all statements made during the performance appraisal. | | | | |
| 20. The performance appraisal process is kept as objective as possible. | | | | |

| Factor | Now Done | Review Needed | Not Relevant | Comments |
|---|---|---|---|---|
| 21. During the performance appraisal, the supervisor should discuss his/her own perspective of progress made by the employee on "problem" points raised during the previous performance appraisal session. | | | | |
| 22. The employee's strong points—as well as weak points—are noted during the performance appraisal. | | | | |
| 23. The supervisor asks employees about their suggestions for improvements during the performance appraisal process. | | | | |
| 24. When applicable, employees are told how to qualify for greater responsibilities during the performance appraisal process. | | | | |
| 25. The supervisor keeps performance appraisal discussions confidential (only the supervisor's own boss is informed about results). | | | | |
| 26. Employees are asked how performance appraisal procedures can be improved. | | | | |
| 27. All company requirements about performance appraisal programs are consistently followed. | | | | |

# 26. Employee Motivation

| Factor | Impact Upon Supervisor | | | Include in Training |
|---|---|---|---|---|
| | Done Consistently | Done Sometimes | Not Done | |
| 1. Employees are told when they have performed good work. | | | | |
| 2. When applicable, employees are involved in the decision-making process regarding matters which pertain to them. | | | | |
| 3. Supervisors are willing to provide some counseling about employees' personal problems. | | | | |
| 4. Employees desiring continuing education opportunities are provided with them. | | | | |
| 5. Qualified employees are promoted to higher-level positions when applicable. | | | | |
| 6. Employee working conditions are reasonable. | | | | |
| 7. Supervisors use a tactful approach when negative discipline is necessary. | | | | |
| 8. Supervisors set a good example for their employees. | | | | |
| 9. Communication freely flows up the organization. | | | | |
| 10. Supervisors support and encourage employee creativity. | | | | |
| 11. Supervisors attempt to assure that "bureaucracy" does not overwhelm efficiency. | | | | |
| 12. Supervisors are trained in effective interpersonal skills. | | | | |
| 13. Supervisors formally recognize individual accomplishments. | | | | |
| 14. Supervisors respect employees' time (schedule, overtime, and other policies are regularly reviewed). | | | | |
| 15. Supervisors promote organizational and employee integrity. | | | | |

| Factor | Impact Upon Supervisor | | | Include in Training |
|---|---|---|---|---|
| | Done Consistently | Done Sometimes | Not Done | |
| 16. Job procedures and standards are defined; employees know how work is to be done. | | | | |
| 17. Employees are provided with effective training opportunities. | | | | |
| 18. Employees know the limits of their—and their supervisor's—authority. | | | | |
| 19. Employees know how their work will be evaluated. | | | | |
| 20. Employees know that their supervisor supports them. | | | | |
| 21. Employees know that their supervisor is interested in them as individuals. | | | | |
| 22. Employees know that their supervisor wants them to succeed. | | | | |
| 23. There are no "favorite" employees. | | | | |
| 24. Employee suggestions are accepted when practical. | | | | |
| 25. There is some humor/fun on the job. | | | | |
| 26. Employee complaints/gripes are promptly investigated; corrective action is taken when applicable. | | | | |
| 27. Employee exit interviews help to discover problems which can be corrected. | | | | |
| 28. Employee grapevine input is considered as personnel decisions are made. | | | | |
| 29. Special attention is given to the effective supervision of young adult workers. | | | | |
| 30. Employees are given challenging work opportunities. | | | | |

# 27. Financial Management (Accounting)

| Factor | Person (Position) Responsible | Comments (Procedural Changes Needed) |
|---|---|---|
| 1. Food service managers have an important role to play in the department's financial management program. | | |
| 2. The food service department head is responsible for developing a departmental operating statement; input is generated from appropriate personnel. | | |
| 3. Systems are in place to budget for and track at least the highest-cost line items. | | |
| 4. Supervisors are responsible for developing applicable sales, inventory, employee, and other reports applicable to their work sections. | | |
| 5. The food service department head knows exactly who is responsible for what part of each line item in the department's budget. | | |
| 6. Sales forecasts for budget purposes are based upon objectively derived information. | | |
| 7. Adequate time is allowed to develop the budget and "numbers" for departmental income statements. | | |
| 8. The food service manager openly requests ideas about ways to improve the financial management program. | | |
| 9. When applicable, the food service department head recognizes that information from staff-level accounting personnel represents advice—not decree. | | |
| 10. Cost items in operating budgets represent reasonable expectations—not just "rounded up numbers" from previous operating periods. | | |
| 11. Income and costs applicable to the food service department are "rolled up" from lower levels in the department. | | |

| Factor | Person (Position) Responsible | Comments (Procedural Changes Needed) |
|---|---|---|
| 12. There is an excellent relationship between the food service department head and applicable personnel in the staff accounting department. | | |
| 13. Budget drafts are developed by personnel in the food service department after broad parameters have been established by top-level management. | | |
| 14. Budget reforecasting is done to update "numbers" developed as the budget was initially planned. | | |
| 15. An objective look is taken at each cost from previous budget periods to confirm that it can be used as a foundation for planning the new budget. (A modified "zero-based" budgeting system is in place.) | | |
| 16. The food service department adheres to a budget calendar, when developed. | | |
| 17. Ongoing studies help assure that, to the extent possible, costs are controlled without sacrificing quality standards. | | |
| 18. Objective procedures are utilized to develop sales forecasts upon which budgets are prepared. | | |
| 19. To the extent practical, all costs are allocated to departments. (There are as few as possible indirect, non-allocated expenses). | | |
| 20. The food service department head is involved in discussions leading to formulas for allocating expenses between departments. | | |
| 21. Supporting schedules are developed to assess labor costs (including benefits) for each section within the department. | | |
| 22. Production standards are in place to help assess labor cost requirements. | | |
| 23. Variance levels have been established which dictate when corrective action must be taken as actual costs exceed budgeted costs. | | |

| Factor | Person (Position) Responsible | Comments (Procedural Changes Needed) |
|---|---|---|
| 24. An accrual (not cash) accounting system is in place within the organization. | | |
| 25. The operating budget is an integral management tool within the food service department; it is not just developed "because it has to be." | | |
| 26. A philosophy is in place which defines profit as an expense; it is not considered to be "what's left over" after all expenses are deducted from income. | | |
| 27. Periodic food costs are determined based upon a "cost of goods" calculation which considers adjustments such as kitchen transfers, employee meal costs, and promotional meal expenditures. | | |
| 28. Budgeted information is used when practical to establish foundations for a pre-cost food control system. | | |
| 29. Profit or "operating surplus" factors are considered as the budget is developed. | | |
| 30. When practical, budgets for each cost/profit center within the food service department should be calculated separately. | | |
| 31. The food service department head has been trained in proper financial management procedures; this training is ongoing. | | |

# 28. Career Development Program

| Factor | Improvement Needed | | If "Yes," Improvement Procedures to Be Used |
|---|---|---|---|
| | Yes | No | |
| 1. The organization and food service department fully support the philosophy of career advancement for qualified employees. | | | |
| 2. A planned program is in place which: | | | |
| a. Identifies employees eligible for career development opportunities. | | | |
| b. Counsels employees on career development opportunities. | | | |
| c. Provides educational opportunities to help employees learn job skills required for advancement. | | | |
| d. Provides reimbursement for qualified educational opportunities. | | | |
| e. Has suggested career ladder channels through the organization. | | | |
| f. Is incorporated into performance evaluation sessions. | | | |
| 3. Knowledge, skills, and experience required for advancement to subsequent positions have been identified for all employees participating in a formalized professional development program. | | | |
| 4. Personal assessment tools are available to interested employees (including managers!) to help them plan their job futures. | | | |
| 5. Periodically, progress toward career goals is discussed with affected employees. | | | |
| 6. A "promotion from within" program is in place when applicable. | | | |
| 7. Job rotation, job enlargement, and/or job enrichment programs are available for interested employees; staff members are encouraged to participate in them. | | | |
| 8. A budget has been established for costs associated with career development activities. | | | |

# 29. Evaluation of Communication

| Factor | Rating | | | | |
|---|---|---|---|---|---|
| | Inadequate | Fair | Acceptable | Good | Exemplary |
| **ORAL PRESENTATION: GENERAL** | | | | | |
| 1. Introduction: Used an effective opening to gain attention; presented a forecast of the presentation. | | | | | |
| 2. Body: Covered all main elements. | | | | | |
| 3. Organization: Presentation was well organized. | | | | | |
| 4. Conclusion included a summary or wrap-up at end. | | | | | |
| 5. Clarity: Used appropriate language and provided adequate explanation of technical aspects, if any. | | | | | |
| 6. Oral Presentation: Spoke clearly, loudly, and neither too quickly nor slowly. | | | | | |
| 7. Appearance/Manner: Used good eye contact; appeared relaxed. | | | | | |
| 8. Use of Visual Aids: Used transparencies, posters, flip charts, and/or handouts. | | | | | |
| 9. Timing: Met required presentation time limit. | | | | | |
| 10. Overall evaluation of presentation. | | | | | |
| **INTERVIEWEE EVALUATION** | | | | | |
| 1. Does person desire to succeed? | | | | | |
| 2. Does person have clear idea of potential value to organization? | | | | | |

| Factor | Rating | | | | |
|---|---|---|---|---|---|
| | Inadequate | Fair | Acceptable | Good | Exemplary |
| 3. Does person show evidence(s) of being aggressive or passive? | | | | | |
| 4. Is person frank? | | | | | |
| 5. Will person likely fit in with the team? | | | | | |
| 6. Does person express beliefs clearly? | | | | | |
| 7. Does person appear open-minded? | | | | | |
| 8. Does person appear to have common sense? | | | | | |
| 9. Does person appear capable of concentration? | | | | | |
| 10. Does person have satisfactory working use of the English language (if necessary)? | | | | | |
| 11. Does person appear capable of organizing work? | | | | | |
| 12. Does person appear to have sufficient initiative (if applicable)? | | | | | |
| 13. Is person tactful? | | | | | |
| 14. Does person have a sense of humor? | | | | | |
| 15. Does person appear to be one who would be a dependable employee? | | | | | |
| **REVISION SCALE FOR ROUTINE LETTERS*** | | | | | |
| **Section 1: Information**<br>1. Primary purpose (main request or idea) is clearly stated. | | | | | |

*Note: The content of this and the remaining three topics of this checklist are from Business Writing Materials (W. Lafayette, IN 1986–1987), Purdue University English 420, pp. 101; 121–122; 139–140; 143–144.

| Factor | Rating | | | | |
|---|---|---|---|---|---|
| | Inadequate | Fair | Acceptable | Good | Exemplary |
| 2. Secondary purposes, such as good will, are achieved. | | | | | |
| 3. Information answers all questions readers may have. | | | | | |
| 4. Reader benefits and individualized detail are included when appropriate. | | | | | |
| **Section 2: Organization: Direct** | | | | | |
| 1. The main idea, request, or question is clearly stated in an opening paragraph. | | | | | |
| 2. Explanations or sub-questions appear in a logical sequence. | | | | | |
| 3. Closing paragraph specifies action when appropriate. | | | | | |
| 4. Enclosures, when necessary, are noted and effectively used. | | | | | |
| 5. Format makes letter readable and attractive. | | | | | |
| **Section 3: Style** | | | | | |
| 1. Style and voice are courteous. | | | | | |
| 2. Language is simple, concise, and correct. | | | | | |
| 3. Sentences emphasize "you" rather than "I" or "we." | | | | | |
| 4. Letter is error-free. | | | | | |

| Factor | Rating | | | | |
|---|---|---|---|---|---|
| | Inadequate | Fair | Acceptable | Good | Exemplary |
| **REVISION SCALE FOR MEMOS** | | | | | |
| **Section 1: Information** | | | | | |
| 1. Primary purpose is clearly stated. | | | | | |
| 2. Secondary purposes—such as building good will or developing rapport—are evident. | | | | | |
| 3. Context/problem and task are carefully defined. | | | | | |
| 4. All information needed to accomplish the solution is presented—in the memo itself or in the attachments. | | | | | |
| **Section 2: Organization** | | | | | |
| 1. The opening segment presents the context/problem, task, and purpose of the memo. | | | | | |
| 2. The summary segment (if needed) presents key findings, conclusions, and recommendations. | | | | | |
| 3. Discussion segments are organized to focus on readers' needs and interests. | | | | | |
| 4. Content moves from general to specific and from most to least important throughout the memo as a whole and within individual segments. | | | | | |
| 5. Attachments (when used) supplement the text, are clearly referenced, and are easy to read. | | | | | |
| 6. Headings indicate the content of individual segments and are parallel in form. | | | | | |

| Factor | Rating | | | | |
|---|---|---|---|---|---|
| | Inadequate | Fair | Acceptable | Good | Exemplary |
| 7. Graphics and lists (when used) simplify reading and are well integrated in the text. | | | | | |
| **Section 3: Style** | | | | | |
| 1. Style and voice are appropriate for decision-making readers, given their organizational roles and relationships to the writer. | | | | | |
| 2. Language is simple, direct, and precise. | | | | | |
| 3. Memo is free of mechanical and grammatical errors. | | | | | |
| **REVISION SCALE FOR PROGRESS REPORTS** | | | | | |
| **Section 1: Information** | | | | | |
| 1. Primary purpose is clearly stated. | | | | | |
| 2. Secondary purposes are achieved. | | | | | |
| 3. Presentation highlights key data, results, conclusions, and/or recommendations to date, plus changes that may have occurred since original proposal. | | | | | |
| 4. Information specifies current research and expected results. | | | | | |
| 5. Plans for future research are clear and specific. | | | | | |
| **Section 2: Organization** | | | | | |
| 1. Opening segment briefly but clearly presents the context/problem, task, and the purpose of the progress report, previewing its content. | | | | | |

| Factor | Rating | | | | |
|---|---|---|---|---|---|
| | Inadequate | Fair | Acceptable | Good | Exemplary |
| 2. Summary segment describes what's been done, mentions key findings, and indicates plans for completing the project by a specified date. | | | | | |
| 3. Discussion segments, organized chronologically or topically, emphasize results and prove progress. | | | | | |
| 4. Each segment presents an overview first, then gives supporting details. | | | | | |
| 5. Closing emphasizes benefits the organization will gain when the project is completed. | | | | | |
| 6. Attachments provide detailed documentation referred to in the text. | | | | | |
| 7. Format, headings, and graphic aids enhance readability. | | | | | |
| **Section 3: Style** 1. Language is simple, concise, and correct. | | | | | |
| 2. Tone and style are appropriate for decision-making readers, given their organizational roles, preferences, and relationships to the writer. | | | | | |
| 3. Report is free of mechanical and grammatical errors. | | | | | |
| **REVISION SCALE FOR LONG OR COMPLEX REPORTS** | | | | | |
| **Section 1: Information** 1. Primary purpose is clearly stated. | | | | | |
| 2. Secondary purposes are effectively achieved but do not bias the report. | | | | | |

| Factor | Rating | | | | |
|---|---|---|---|---|---|
| | Inadequate | Fair | Acceptable | Good | Exemplary |
| 3. Information enables readers to see how the report meets organizational needs. | | | | | |
| 4. Information responds to the professional needs (and personal attitudes) of primary and secondary readers. | | | | | |
| 5. Detailed information is complete; there are no unanswered questions or open loops. | | | | | |
| 6. Information enables readers to understand conclusions, to accept recommendations, and to find what they need to do their own work. | | | | | |
| **Section 2: Organization** | | | | | |
| 1. Presentation moves from general to particular and from most to least important in the report and in individual segments. | | | | | |
| 2. Transmittal letter or memo presents the context/problem, assignment or task, and purpose of the report; it highlights key results, conclusions, and recommendations; and it ends courteously. | | | | | |
| 3. Discussion has an introduction, body, and conclusion, and is clearly segmented. | | | | | |
| 4. Detailed research findings and/or sources are presented in the appendices, reference, and bibliography. | | | | | |
| 5. Cover, title page, table of contents, format signals, and graphics make the report accessible and useful to readers. | | | | | |

| Factor | Rating | | | | |
|---|---|---|---|---|---|
| | Inadequate | Fair | Acceptable | Good | Exemplary |
| **Section 3: Style** 1. Voice is appropriate to readers and purposes. | | | | | |
| 2. Language is simple, concise, and correct. | | | | | |
| 3. Report is free of grammatical and mechanical distractions. | | | | | |

# 30. Delegation

| Factor | Impact Upon Supervisor | | | Include in Training |
|---|---|---|---|---|
| | Done Consistently | Done Sometimes | Not Done | |
| 1. Management personnel philosophy supports the concept of delegation to qualified subordinates. | | | | |
| 2. Managers recognize that ultimate responsibility for job performance cannot be delegated. | | | | |
| 3. Managers recognize that the authority (power) necessary to do delegated work must be given to the affected subordinate. | | | | |
| 4. Managers do not delegate priority activities; they do delegate those activities which can reasonably be performed by a subordinate. | | | | |
| 5. Managers recognize that they need free time on the job and personal time away from the job; they recognize that delegation is a way to accomplish these needs. | | | | |
| 6. Managers consider delegating tasks which are routine, trivial, highly specialized, and those which are "choice" or "pet" projects. | | | | |
| 7. Managers know that they cannot delegate tasks which involve policy-making, specific personnel matters, crises, or other activities which involve confidential matters. | | | | |
| 8. Managers know what their subordinates are capable of and utilize this information as delegation decisions are made. | | | | |
| 9. Delegation is not taken for granted; follow-up monitoring activities are still typically required. | | | | |
| 10. Food service managers delegate as an integral part of an employee's professional development program. | | | | |
| 11. After delegated tasks are completed, credit is given to the responsible employee. | | | | |

| Factor | Impact Upon Supervisor | | | Include in Training |
|---|---|---|---|---|
| | Done Consistently | Done Sometimes | Not Done | |
| 12. When delegating, time frames and factors which will be used to evaluate completed work must be discussed. | | | | |
| 13. Employees are given all necessary information, tools, time and/or other resources required to successfully complete the delegated assignment. | | | | |
| 14. Employees to whom work has been delegated know that managers are willing to provide advice and counsel as unexpected or other problems evolve. | | | | |
| 15. When applicable, focus on results of the delegated task—not the methods which should be used to "get there." | | | | |
| 16. Managers openly discuss all aspects of the task to be delegated and encourage ongoing dialogue to ensure problems do not arise. | | | | |
| 17. Specific deadlines (final and interim) for task completion are part of the delegated assignment. | | | | |
| 18. Normally, an entire task should be delegated to one individual rather than "splitting it up" among staff members. | | | | |
| 19. Food service managers emphasize the importance of delegation; they do not build obstacles which prevent it. | | | | |
| 20. Food service managers are knowledgeable about the work that they should—and should not—do, and do not "over-delegate" to one or more staff members. | | | | |

# 31. Orientation Topics (Initial Training and Handbook)

| Factor | Important | | If "Yes" | |
|---|---|---|---|---|
| | No | Yes | Currently Included | Need |
| **Introduction: Welcome** | | | | |
| 1. Organizational (Property) Philosophy. | | | | |
| 2. Opportunities with Organization (Property). | | | | |
| 3. Emphasis on Guest. | | | | |
| 4. Employment Advancement Opportunity Program. | | | | |
| 5. Probationary Period. | | | | |
| 6. Suggestions. | | | | |
| **Section 1: Hours, Pay, Vacations, and Time Off** | | | | |
| 1. Work Schedules (Attendance). | | | | |
| 2. Overtime. | | | | |
| 3. Wage and Salary Reviews. | | | | |
| 4. Pay Day and Deductions from Pay. | | | | |
| 5. Vacations. | | | | |
| 6. Paid Holidays. | | | | |
| 7. Absence. | | | | |
| 8. Punctuality. | | | | |
| 9. Time Off. | | | | |
| 10. Wage Attachments. | | | | |
| 11. Tipping. | | | | |

| Factor | Important | | If "Yes" | |
|---|---|---|---|---|
| | No | Yes | Currently Included | Need |
| 12. Jury Duty Pay. | | | | |
| 13. Layoff Policy. | | | | |
| **Section 2: Employee Benefits** | | | | |
| 1. Sick Leave and Disability Plan (Hourly Employees). | | | | |
| 2. Sick Leave and Disability Plan (Salaried Employees). | | | | |
| 3. Social Security Disability Benefits. | | | | |
| 4. Medical Certification and General. | | | | |
| 5. Insurance Coverages (Non-union Employees). | | | | |
| 6. Comprehensive Medical Expense Benefits. | | | | |
| 7. Dental and Vision Care Expense Benefits. | | | | |
| 8. General Information. | | | | |
| 9. Funeral Leave. | | | | |
| 10. Meals and Uniforms. | | | | |
| **Section 3: Retirement Income** | | | | |
| 1. Pension Plan. | | | | |
| 2. Retirement Dates. | | | | |
| 3. Vested Benefits. | | | | |
| 4. Death Benefits. | | | | |

| Factor | Important | | If "Yes" | |
|---|---|---|---|---|
| | No | Yes | Currently Included | Need |
| 5. Income. | | | | |
| 6. Method of Payment. | | | | |
| 7. Illustration of Pension Plan Benefits. | | | | |
| 8. Social Security. | | | | |
| **Section 4: Safety Guides** | | | | |
| 1. Safety, Health and Security. | | | | |
| 2. Accidents. | | | | |
| 3. Safekeeping of Personal Property. | | | | |
| 4. Fire/Civil Defense. | | | | |
| 5. Purse/Package Inspection | | | | |
| 6. Security Investigation-Inquiry. | | | | |
| **Section 5: Personal Guidelines** | | | | |
| 1. Appearance and Dress. | | | | |
| 2. Emergency Procedures. | | | | |
| 3. Licensing and Work Permit. | | | | |
| 4. Employee Recognition Program. | | | | |
| 5. Employee Publication(s). | | | | |
| 6. Grievance Procedures. | | | | |
| 7. Criminal Offenses. | | | | |

| Factor | Important | | If "Yes" | |
| --- | --- | --- | --- | --- |
| | No | Yes | Currently Included | Need |
| 8. Work Area. | | | | |
| 9. Outside Employment. | | | | |
| 10. Identification Required for Work. | | | | |
| 11. Telephones. | | | | |
| 12. Standards of Conduct. | | | | |
| 13. Telephone Manners. | | | | |
| 14. Recreational/Social Activity. | | | | |
| 15. Personal Correspondence. | | | | |
| 16. Visitors. | | | | |
| 17. Name Badges. | | | | |
| 18. Lunch Periods. | | | | |
| 19. Personal Records and Procedures. | | | | |
| 20. Seniority. | | | | |
| 21. Differences of Opinion, Personal Problems, Grievances. | | | | |
| 22. Service Recognition. | | | | |
| 23. Education. | | | | |
| 24. Personal Property. | | | | |
| 25. Orientation. | | | | |
| 26. On-the-Job Training. | | | | |

| Factor | Important | | If "Yes" | |
|---|---|---|---|---|
| | No | Yes | Currently Included | Need |
| 27. Package Inspection. | | | | |
| 28. Tuition Refund Program. | | | | |
| 29. Parking. | | | | |
| 30. Performance Appraisal Procedures. | | | | |
| **Section 6: Rules of Conduct** <br> 1. Equipment or Property. | | | | |
| 2. Conduct (Discipline) | | | | |
| 3. Attendance. | | | | |
| 4. Job Performance. | | | | |

## 32. Multi-Cultural Management

| Factor | Relevance | | If High Relevance | | | | Comments |
|---|---|---|---|---|---|---|---|
| | Low | High | No Action Needed | Need to Learn More | Use in Management Training | Revise Policy/ Procedure | |
| **Section 1: Background Information** | | | | | | | |
| 1. The operation (property) will benefit from management's study of multi-cultural factors: | | | | | | | |
| a. Managers can examine their attitudes and beliefs. | | | | | | | |
| b. Managers can better know about social factors affecting society. | | | | | | | |
| c. Managers will learn alternative tactics for dealing with people. | | | | | | | |
| d. There will be less institutional and personal prejudice. | | | | | | | |
| 2. Participation in relationships on and off the job are often influenced by ethnic considerations. | | | | | | | |
| 3. All managers should study the role which ethnicity plays in American society and culture. | | | | | | | |
| 4. One's attachment and identity with one's ethnic group varies greatly with the individual; it may or may not be a significant concern. | | | | | | | |

| Factor | Relevance | | No Action Needed | If High Relevance | | | Comments |
|---|---|---|---|---|---|---|---|
| | Low | High | | Need to Learn More | Use in Management Training | Revise Policy/ Procedure | |
| 5. Members of ethnic minority groups are often victims of racism and stereotypes and are often members of lower socioeconomic classes. | | | | | | | |
| 6. It is helpful to know how one is viewed from the perspective of those in other cultures. | | | | | | | |
| 7. An emphasis on conformity (suppressing adversity between cultural groups) is typically unproductive. | | | | | | | |
| 8. A work ethnic which criticizes leisure is not shared by all cultures | | | | | | | |
| 9. One should not justify one value system by implicitly rejecting/ignoring those of others. | | | | | | | |
| 10. There may be no real relationship between images associated with a stereotype and predominant traits of a specific cultural group. | | | | | | | |
| 11. The culture of a minority group changes as it comes in contact with other cultures. | | | | | | | |
| 12. Words and phrases have different meanings; the same phrases may be complimentary/insulting when used with different groups. | | | | | | | |

| Factor | Relevance | | If High Relevance | | | | Comments |
|---|---|---|---|---|---|---|---|
| | Low | High | No Action Needed | Need to Learn More | Use in Management Training | Revise Policy/ Procedure | |
| 13. Bilingual competence may be considered an advantage or handicap. | | | | | | | |
| 14. A native language may have little—or great—functionality in the work place. | | | | | | | |
| 15. Gestures/postures/eye contact may be more or less significant in different cultures. | | | | | | | |
| 16. To whom, when, and about what one may talk vary among cultures. | | | | | | | |
| 17. Behaviors which are socially acceptable (and unacceptable) differ between employees from different cultures. | | | | | | | |
| 18. Matters that are considered sacred and secular differ between cultures. | | | | | | | |
| 19. Dietary restrictions may be an integral part of some religions/cultures. | | | | | | | |
| 20. Beliefs about illness and death, responsibility for curing, treatment for specific illnesses, etc., vary significantly among ethnic groups. | | | | | | | |

| Factor | Relevance | | If High Relevance | | | | Comments |
|---|---|---|---|---|---|---|---|
| | Low | High | No Action Needed | Need to Learn More | Use in Management Training | Revise Policy/ Procedure | |
| 21. Beliefs or practices about body hygiene (such as bathing frequency) are not the same in all ethnic groups. | | | | | | | |
| 22. Food, including its definition, is of enormous social significance, and beliefs and practices about food vary greatly among cultures. | | | | | | | |
| 23. Dress and personal appearance concerns can create many cross-cultural problems. | | | | | | | |
| 24. Matters of history, tradition and pride vary among ethnic groups. | | | | | | | |
| 25. Holidays and celebrations differ among cultures. | | | | | | | |
| 26. The purpose, priority and methods of education vary greatly in different cultures. | | | | | | | |
| 27. The definition of what is "work" and "play" is dissimilar among cultural groups. | | | | | | | |
| 28. The kinds of work that are prestigious (and reasons for the prestige) vary among cultural groups. | | | | | | | |

| Factor | Relevance | | If High Relevance | | | | Comments |
|---|---|---|---|---|---|---|---|
| | Low | High | No Action Needed | Need to Learn More | Use in Management Training | Revise Policy/ Procedure | |
| 29. Reasons for the value of work (financial gain, group welfare, individual satisfaction, etc.) differ among cultures. | | | | | | | |
| 30. There are many stereotypes about what work groups will—and will not—do. | | | | | | | |
| 31. Beliefs and values associated with time (such as punctuality) and space (such as how individuals group together) differ among cultures. | | | | | | | |
| 32. Beliefs and practices about natural phenomena (such as the sun and moon, lightning, earthquakes, etc.) have great significance to and variations among different cultures. | | | | | | | |
| **Section 2: Management Practices in the Work Place** | | | | | | | |
| 1. Cultural conflict is a critical factor in the success or failure of business. | | | | | | | |
| 2. Successful and ongoing interpersonal relationships between managers and employees are important. | | | | | | | |
| 3. Successful managers perceive that different social customs interact when employees of multi-cultural backgrounds work together. | | | | | | | |

| Factor | Relevance | | If High Relevance | | | | Comments |
|---|---|---|---|---|---|---|---|
| | Low | High | No Action Needed | Need to Learn More | Use in Management Training | Revise Policy/Procedure | |
| 4. Some degree of conflict between different social systems may be inevitable. | | | | | | | |
| 5. Many work-related behaviors exhibited by ethnically different employees are culturally determined. | | | | | | | |
| 6. Managers need to know what significant questions to address about cultural differences between ethnic groups. | | | | | | | |
| 7. Managers must understand the basic values and beliefs of employees in different cultural groups. | | | | | | | |
| 8. Managers must know how to minimize conflict caused by differences in ethnic backgrounds and, when found to exist, must be able to channel it toward constructive purposes. | | | | | | | |
| 9. Points of potential conflict among different ethnic groups and life styles can—and should—be identified and managed. | | | | | | | |
| 10. Managers know that when different social systems exist three types of conflict are common: <br> a. Procedural conflicts (disagreements about courses of action). | | | | | | | |

| Factor | Relevance | | If High Relevance | | | | Comments |
|---|---|---|---|---|---|---|---|
| | Low | High | No Action Needed | Need to Learn More | Use in Management Training | Revise Policy/ Procedure | |
| b. Substantive conflicts (stemming from incompatible goals). | | | | | | | |
| c. Interpersonal conflicts arise when different attitudes, beliefs, and values are held by different individuals. | | | | | | | |
| 11. When employees with different ethnic backgrounds have conflict on the job they can: | | | | | | | |
| a. Meet job-related needs—which often causes personal frustration. | | | | | | | |
| b. Satisfy individual needs—which can lead to unsatisfactory work. | | | | | | | |
| c. Receive help from their supervisor so that reasonable comparisons between their job and individual needs can be addressed. | | | | | | | |
| 12. The more that one retains an ethnic identity, the greater the likelihood that there will be cultural conflict at work. | | | | | | | |
| 13. Not all members of a specific ethnic group think and react the same way about any specific issue on the job. | | | | | | | |

| Factor | Relevance | | If High Relevance | | | | Comments |
|---|---|---|---|---|---|---|---|
| | Low | High | No Action Needed | Need to Learn More | Use in Management Training | Revise Policy/Procedure | |
| 14. A manager earns respect by relating to each employee individually, to the extent practical. | | | | | | | |
| 15. The manager gains respect when he/she demonstrates acceptable behavior to subordinates. | | | | | | | |
| 16. The manager may encourage employees to strive for self-directed goals. | | | | | | | |
| 17. The manager should arrange training time to work with employees of like ethnic groups in individualized situations. | | | | | | | |
| 18. Managers must be sensitive to all employees' needs for specialized assistance. | | | | | | | |
| 19. The manager should make efforts to avoid placing employees in positions which encourage them to disagree with management personnel. | | | | | | | |
| 20. The manager can play "devil's advocate" to stimulate independent thinking. | | | | | | | |
| 21. Small group situations in which employees can interrelate should be encouraged. | | | | | | | |

| Factor | Relevance | | If High Relevance | | | | Comments |
|---|---|---|---|---|---|---|---|
| | Low | High | No Action Needed | Need to Learn More | Use in Management Training | Revise Policy/ Procedure | |
| 22. Individualized learning and tutoring situations can be helpful in recognizing individual differences in the training/working environment. | | | | | | | |
| 23. The manager should recognized that the minority employee may be experiencing "cultural shock" if the job is timed with recent arrival in this country. | | | | | | | |
| 24. Managers recognize that those with different perceptions, thought and speech patterns and behavior are not "wrong" or "unnatural." | | | | | | | |
| 25. Managers recognize that, despite intelligence and the best of intentions, people cannot "automatically" function effectively out of their predominant culture. | | | | | | | |
| 26. Managers recognize that people *can* learn how to function in different cultures. | | | | | | | |
| 27. Managers recognize that people can develop skills helpful in interacting with persons from other cultures. | | | | | | | |
| 28. Managers are aware of their own values, assumptions, needs and limitations. | | | | | | | |
| 29. Managers practice cultural-reading (in efforts to note the inherent logic in other cultures). | | | | | | | |

| Factor | Relevance | | If High Relevance | | | | Comments |
|---|---|---|---|---|---|---|---|
| | Low | High | No Action Needed | Need to Learn More | Use in Management Training | Revise Policy/ Procedure | |
| 30. Managers are able to objectively assess situations from other perspectives. | | | | | | | |
| 31. Managers are able to effectively send/receive messages to/from those of other cultures. | | | | | | | |
| 32. Managers are able to readjust their expectations based upon the employees they supervise. | | | | | | | |
| 33. Managers can monitor their own adjustment to a new culture. | | | | | | | |
| 34. Managers can relate to others from a different culture. | | | | | | | |
| 35. Monetary and human costs associated with not providing intercultural training are recognized. | | | | | | | |
| 36. When practical, managers receive training in basic language instruction, general cultural concepts, and how to assist employees with culture shock. | | | | | | | |
| 37. Ongoing management development programs include component(s) relating to intercultural information. | | | | | | | |

| Factor | Relevance | | No Action Needed | If High Relevance | | | Comments |
|---|---|---|---|---|---|---|---|
| | Low | High | | Need to Learn More | Use in Management Training | Revise Policy/ Procedure | |
| 38. Managers who have difficulty in effectively supervising cultural minorities are given additional training. | | | | | | | |
| 39. Managers understand the expectations of cultural minorities. | | | | | | | |
| **Section 3: Managers Understand the Following** | | | | | | | |
| 1. It is not necessary to prove a right to leadership in many cultures (authority is inherited and is vested in a person, not in a position). | | | | | | | |
| 2. It is generally important that managers behave appropriately (from the employees' perspective) for the management role. | | | | | | | |
| 3. There are signals of rank which suggest power/authority; these differ between cultures. | | | | | | | |
| 4. It is typically important for managers to show strong personal concern for employees and guests. | | | | | | | |
| 5. Often managers must devote significant amounts of time to personal contacts with employees. | | | | | | | |

| Factor | Relevance | | No Action Needed | If High Relevance | | | Comments |
|---|---|---|---|---|---|---|---|
| | Low | High | | Need to Learn More | Use in Management Training | Revise Policy/ Procedure | |
| 6. It is generally not useful for managers to provide selected information to only some subordinates; all employees at the same organizational level should be given the same information. | | | | | | | |
| 7. Managers understand that employees in some cultures (South American, European, and European-influenced, for example) often do not expect an opportunity to provide input to the decision-making process. | | | | | | | |
| 8. Managers realize why supervisory efforts with cultural immigrants often fail; there can be: | | | | | | | |
| a. Lack of understanding about the culture. | | | | | | | |
| b. Failure to learn employees' expectations. | | | | | | | |
| c. Inability to effectively relate to workers. | | | | | | | |
| d. Failure to verify information. | | | | | | | |
| e. Arrogance. | | | | | | | |
| f. Unwillingness to listen. | | | | | | | |

| Factor | Relevance | | If High Relevance | | | | Comments |
|---|---|---|---|---|---|---|---|
| | Low | High | No Action Needed | Need to Learn More | Use in Management Training | Revise Policy/ Procedure | |
| g. "Conversation problems." | | | | | | | |
| h. Changing strategies too frequently. | | | | | | | |
| i. Too much/too little trust in others. | | | | | | | |
| 9. Managers must understand the employees' definition/philosophy/attitude about "work ethics." | | | | | | | |
| 10. It is important to be sensitive to inter group hostilities and social practices. | | | | | | | |
| 11. Incentives/rewards must be considered for appropriateness from the perspective of the affected employees. | | | | | | | |
| 12. Managers have patience and a willingness to permit foreign employees to make some mistakes. | | | | | | | |
| 13. Public criticism of an employee is not an acceptable practice; preservation of dignity is very important. | | | | | | | |
| 14. "Courteous explanation" is typically the best way to enforce employee standards for persons in many cultures. | | | | | | | |

| Factor | Relevance | | No Action Needed | If High Relevance | | | Comments |
|---|---|---|---|---|---|---|---|
| | Low | High | | Need to Learn More | Use in Management Training | Revise Policy/ Procedure | |
| 15. There is an ongoing need for close supervisory follow-up as employees perform required work tasks. | | | | | | | |
| 16. Managers realize that employees from many cultures do not have values which prohibit bribery, pilfering equipment, neglect, absenteeism, etc. | | | | | | | |
| 17. Managers know that, as with the American culture, trainability rather than experience may be most important to job success. | | | | | | | |
| 18. Managers understand that employees from many cultures will, by American standards, be too modest; this may impact upon recruitment/selection decisions. | | | | | | | |

# Part VI | Food Service Management Priorities

# 33. Guest Relations

| Factor | In Use (✓) | Corrective Action Required | | | | | Assigned To | Compliance Date |
|---|---|---|---|---|---|---|---|---|
| | | Develop | | Closer Supervision | Training Needed | Other (Describe) | | |
| | | Procedure | Policy | | | | | |
| 1. Management has a written statement about its concern for guest service; the "philosophy" of guest service is integral to all orientation/training activities. | | | | | | | | |
| 2. Procedures are designed to focus on "what's best" for the guest. | | | | | | | | |
| 3. Management has developed a well-conceived strategy for service. | | | | | | | | |
| 4. Employees are trained to keep their attention focused on guests' needs. | | | | | | | | |
| 5. Top management is committed to guest service in both words and deeds. | | | | | | | | |
| 6. Managers use a questioning process to determine what their guests want and need—and how the organization can meet or exceed these needs. | | | | | | | | |
| 7. Employees are taught to smile and be friendly at all times. | | | | | | | | |

| Factor | In Use (✓) | Corrective Action Required | | | | | Assigned To | Compliance Date |
| | | Develop | | Closer Supervision | Training Needed | Other (Describe) | | |
| | | Procedure | Policy | | | | | |
|---|---|---|---|---|---|---|---|---|
| 8. Employees are taught to reinforce the guests' feelings of self-worth. | | | | | | | | |
| 9. Employees can "communicate" their genuine interest in helping the guests. | | | | | | | | |
| 10. Employees provide fast and courteous service. | | | | | | | | |
| 11. Employees have been trained in teamwork practices which focus on the guests. | | | | | | | | |
| 12. Employees have a feeling of being a "professional" and of being important to the organization and the guests. | | | | | | | | |
| 13. Employees are taught to anticipate problems—not to wait until guests complain. | | | | | | | | |
| 14. Employees are knowledgeable about how work should be done and consistently meet job-related standards. | | | | | | | | |

| Factor | In Use (✓) | Corrective Action Required | | | | | | Assigned To | Compliance Date |
|---|---|---|---|---|---|---|---|---|---|
| | | Develop | | Closer Supervision | Training Needed | Other (Describe) | | | |
| | | Procedure | Policy | | | | | | |
| 15. Employees provide proper answers to all guests' questions—or alert their supervisor when additional information is necessary. | | | | | | | | | |
| 16. Employees consistently wear the appropriate uniform which is kept clean and neat. | | | | | | | | | |
| 17. Employees know when to contact their supervisor about potential conflict situations involving guests. | | | | | | | | | |
| 18. Employees are aware of the philosophy of treating guests the way they want to be treated. | | | | | | | | | |
| 19. Employees are taught not to divide guests into categories of those whom they "like" and "dislike." | | | | | | | | | |
| 20. When practical, employees provide their undivided interest to the needs and concerns of guests. | | | | | | | | | |
| 21. Employees consistently practice the manners and social courtesy due all persons. | | | | | | | | | |

| Factor | In Use (√) | Corrective Action Required | | | | | Assigned To | Compliance Date |
| | | Develop | | Closer Supervision | Training Needed | Other (Describe) | | |
| | | Procedure | Policy | | | | | |
|---|---|---|---|---|---|---|---|---|
| 22. Employees understand that guests do not care about their—or the company's—problems; employees focus on trying to help the customers. | | | | | | | | |
| 23. Applicable personnel are taught the proper procedures to handle guests' complaints. | | | | | | | | |
| 24. Employees are taught to maintain good "eye-to-eye" contact when speaking with guests. | | | | | | | | |
| 25. Employees try to accommodate any special guest needs. | | | | | | | | |
| 26. Employees recognize guests immediately even if they are busy; they indicate how long it will be until service can be rendered. | | | | | | | | |
| 27. Applicable employees are taught procedures of telephone "etiquette." | | | | | | | | |
| 28. Guests are thanked for visiting the property. | | | | | | | | |

| Factor | In Use (✓) | Corrective Action Required | | | | | | Assigned To | Compliance Date |
| | | Develop | | Closer Supervision | Training Needed | Other (Describe) | | | |
| | | Procedure | Policy | | | | | | |
|---|---|---|---|---|---|---|---|---|---|
| 29. When applicable, guests' names are used by employees. | | | | | | | | | |
| 30. Employees pay attention to details regarding all work that they do. | | | | | | | | | |

153

## 34. Sanitation

| Factor | In Use (✓) | Corrective Action Required | | | | | | Assigned To | Compliance Date |
|---|---|---|---|---|---|---|---|---|---|
| | | Develop | | Closer Supervision | Training Needed | Other (Describe) | | | |
| | | Procedure | Policy | | | | | | |
| 1. All personnel are trained in effective personal hygiene practices. | | | | | | | | | |
| 2. Supervisors confirm that personal hygiene requirements of the property are met by all personnel on all shifts. | | | | | | | | | |
| 3. Personnel are not allowed to smoke or chew gum in food storage, production, service, or cleanup areas. | | | | | | | | | |
| 4. Proper handwashing facilities are available in convenient locations. | | | | | | | | | |
| 5. Food products are always purchased from reliable and approved sources. | | | | | | | | | |
| 6. Only commercially processed canned foods are used. | | | | | | | | | |
| 7. Dry storage areas are kept clean, dry, well-ventilated, and at temperatures between 50°F and 70°F. | | | | | | | | | |

| Factor | In Use (✓) | Corrective Action Required | | | | | Assigned To | Compliance Date |
|---|---|---|---|---|---|---|---|---|
| | | Develop | | Closer Supervision | Training Needed | Other (Describe) | | |
| | | Procedure | Policy | | | | | |
| 8. Shelving and storage units are slatted, kept at least one inch away from the wall, and four to six inches off the floor to facilitate cleaning. | | | | | | | | |
| 9. Poisons, toxic materials and cleaning supplies are not stored in food storage/preparation areas. | | | | | | | | |
| 10. Refrigerated storage areas are maintained at a temperature below 40°. | | | | | | | | |
| 11. All food items are covered before storing. | | | | | | | | |
| 12. Freezer storage areas are maintained between 0°F and –10°F. | | | | | | | | |
| 13. When possible, frozen foods are stored in their original packing containers; when this is not possible, moisture/vapor proof materials are used. | | | | | | | | |
| 14. Frozen foods which have been thawed are not refrozen. | | | | | | | | |

| Factor | In Use (√) | Corrective Action Required | | | | | Assigned To | Compliance Date |
| | | Develop | | Closer Supervision | Training Needed | Other (Describe) | | |
| | | Procedure | Policy | | | | | |
|---|---|---|---|---|---|---|---|---|
| 15. Cans that have swelling, dents, off-odors, or foam/milkiness of juice are not used. | | | | | | | | |
| 16. Meats that have off-odors and slimy surfaces are not used. | | | | | | | | |
| 17. Single service/disposable plastic gloves are used when food is handled extensively. | | | | | | | | |
| 18. Equipment/utensils used in preparing/serving food are kept clean. | | | | | | | | |
| 19. Food contact surfaces of equipment/tables used to prepare raw foods are completely cleaned before being used to handle cooked food. | | | | | | | | |
| 20. Raw fruit/vegetables are thoroughly washed before preparation/serving. | | | | | | | | |
| 21. Perishable foods are prepared as close to serving time as possible. | | | | | | | | |

| Factor | In Use (√) | Corrective Action Required | | | | | | Assigned To | Compliance Date |
|---|---|---|---|---|---|---|---|---|---|
| | | Develop | | Closer Supervision | Training Needed | Other (Describe) | | | |
| | | Procedure | Policy | | | | | | |
| 22. Potentially hazardous foods (those high in protein content) are handled with extreme care; time is minimized during which these products are kept within the "danger" temperature zone of 40°F to 140°F. | | | | | | | | | |
| 23. Protein-rich foods are cooled rapidly; they are placed in shallow pans, are refrigerated immediately, and otherwise are carefully handled. | | | | | | | | | |
| 24. Frozen foods are not thawed by leaving at room temperature. | | | | | | | | | |
| 25. All applicable laws and policies relating to the washing of pots and pans, tableware, cooking utensils, etc., are consistently followed. | | | | | | | | | |
| 26. Eating utensils are carefully handled by service and ware-washing personnel. | | | | | | | | | |
| 27. When practical, dishes, flatware, and other eating utensils are allowed to air dry; they are not towel dried. | | | | | | | | | |
| 28. The proper serving utensils are used; food is not touched by employees' hands. | | | | | | | | | |

| Factor | In Use (√) | Corrective Action Required | | | | | | Assigned To | Compliance Date |
|---|---|---|---|---|---|---|---|---|---|
| | | Develop | | Closer Supervision | Training Needed | Other (Describe) | | | |
| | | Procedure | Policy | | | | | | |
| 29. All personnel are properly trained in the proper, sanitary production and service of foods; practices which are taught are consistently used. | | | | | | | | | |
| 30. Detailed facility and equipment cleaning schedules are available and are used. | | | | | | | | | |

158

# 35. Safety

| Factor | In Use (√) | Corrective Action Required | | | | | Assigned To | Compliance Date |
|---|---|---|---|---|---|---|---|---|
| | | Develop | | Closer Supervision | Training Needed | Other (Describe) | | |
| | | Procedure | Policy | | | | | |
| 1. Dry potholders are always used to handle hot utensils. | | | | | | | | |
| 2. Handles of pots and pans do not protrude into traffic aisles. | | | | | | | | |
| 3. Manufacturers' instructions are consistently followed for all equipment. | | | | | | | | |
| 4. Glass containers and other glass items are not permitted in kitchen areas. | | | | | | | | |
| 5. Proper procedures for lifting heavy items are consistently followed. | | | | | | | | |
| 6. Floors are kept clean and dry at all times; spills are wiped up immediately. | | | | | | | | |
| 7. Personnel wear low-heeled, properly fitting shoes with non-skid soles; the heels and toes are completely enclosed. | | | | | | | | |
| 8. Personnel have been trained in the safe way to handle knives. | | | | | | | | |

159

| Factor | In Use (√) | Corrective Action Required | | | | | Assigned To | Compliance Date |
|---|---|---|---|---|---|---|---|---|
| | | Develop | | Closer Supervision | Training Needed | Other (Describe) | | |
| | | Procedure | Policy | | | | | |
| 9. When applicable, equipment is always unplugged before cleaning. | | | | | | | | |
| 10. A qualified electrician inspects all electrical equipment, wiring, switches, etc., on a regularly scheduled, preventive maintenance basis. | | | | | | | | |
| 11. The proper fire extinguishing equipment is available; it is regularly inspected and maintained. | | | | | | | | |
| 12. Local fire authorities are consulted about applicable fire prevention practices. | | | | | | | | |
| 13. Personnel have been trained in proper procedures used to put out fires. | | | | | | | | |
| 14. Adequate lighting is available in all working areas. | | | | | | | | |
| 15. All food service equipment is regularly inspected and kept in good repair. | | | | | | | | |

| Factor | In Use (√) | Corrective Action Required | | | | | Assigned To | Compliance Date |
|---|---|---|---|---|---|---|---|---|
| | | Develop | | Closer Supervision | Training Needed | Other (Describe) | | |
| | | Procedure | Policy | | | | | |
| 16. Instruction from equipment manufacturers for proper equipment operation are incorporated into orientation and ongoing training programs for all staff. | | | | | | | | |
| 17. Management staff make frequent inspection of facilities to identify and correct safety hazards. | | | | | | | | |
| 18. All accidents are investigated and reported to appropriate officials. | | | | | | | | |
| 19. Preventive action is taken when accidents occur to help assure that they do not recur. | | | | | | | | |
| 20. Personnel are trained to promptly notify their supervisor when potential safety problems are noticed. | | | | | | | | |
| 21. All unsafe work conditions are corrected as soon as possible. | | | | | | | | |
| 22. Personnel are trained in basic medical treatment procedures; they know when expert help is needed. | | | | | | | | |

| Factor | In Use (√) | Corrective Action Required | | | | | Assigned To | Compliance Date |
|---|---|---|---|---|---|---|---|---|
| | | Develop | | Closer Supervision | Training Needed | Other (Describe) | | |
| | | Procedure | Policy | | | | | |
| 23. First-aid kits meeting all local requirements are readily available. | | | | | | | | |
| 24. Detailed safety checklists are used to help inspect food service facilities.* | | | | | | | | |
| 25. Safety is stressed at all training and other applicable meetings. | | | | | | | | |
| 26. Personnel are trained in procedures to be followed if accidents occur to guests. | | | | | | | | |
| 27. The facility is, at all times, maintained according to standards required by local ordinances. | | | | | | | | |
| 28. Personnel are aware of procedures to be followed in case of fires, bomb scares, robberies, and other potential problems. | | | | | | | | |
| 29. Insurance carriers are consulted regarding suggestions to improve the safety of guests, employees, and the facility itself. | | | | | | | | |

*See, for example, *Safety Operations Manual*, National Restaurant Association (Chicago, IL: No date).

# 36. Cash Collection Procedures

| Factor | In Use (√) | Corrective Action Required | | | | | | Assigned To | Compliance Date |
|---|---|---|---|---|---|---|---|---|---|
| | | Develop | | Closer Supervision | Training Needed | Other (Describe) | | | |
| | | Procedure | Policy | | | | | | |
| 1. No food products can be received from personnel in the kitchen/bar unless they have first been entered into a sales income system including order entry on a guest check. | | | | | | | | | |
| 2. A system is in place to match items sold (revenues collected) with items produced. | | | | | | | | | |
| 3. When practical, production and service staff work on rotating schedules to minimize opportunities for collusion. | | | | | | | | | |
| 4. Service staff are held accountable for all guest checks (unless selected computer systems negate the need for this). | | | | | | | | | |
| 5. All guest checks are accounted for at the end of each service shift (unless specialized computer systems negate the need for this). | | | | | | | | | |
| 6. Unless specialized computer systems are used, guest checks are randomly and routinely checked for arithmetic, pricing, and other errors. | | | | | | | | | |

| Factor | In Use (√) | Develop Procedure | Develop Policy | Closer Supervision | Training Needed | Other (Describe) | Assigned To | Compliance Date |
|---|---|---|---|---|---|---|---|---|
| | | | | Corrective Action Required | | | | |
| 7. Careful records are kept to monitor the number of guest "walkouts" on a by-server basis. | | | | | | | | |
| 8. Unless selected computerized systems are used, all guest checks are carefully kept secure. (Personnel do not have access to them.) | | | | | | | | |
| 9. If transfers of guest changes between lounge/restaurant areas are permitted, careful record keeping procedures help assure that all income due from guests is actually collected. | | | | | | | | |
| 10. A detailed listing of standard operating procedures for used of electronic data machines (cash registers) is available and is consistently used; close supervision helps assure that procedures are always followed. | | | | | | | | |
| 12. When a duplicate guest check system is in use, kitchen copies are checked with the servers' hard copies. | | | | | | | | |

| Factor | In Use (√) | Develop Procedure | Develop Policy | Closer Supervision | Training Needed | Other (Describe) | Assigned To | Compliance Date |
|---|---|---|---|---|---|---|---|---|
| | | | | Corrective Action Required | | | | |
| 13. An effective sales income control system is in place so that the amount of funds which should be in the register can be checked with what is actually available. | | | | | | | | |
| 14. Petty cash—not register "payouts"—are used for small cash purchases; an easy "audit trail" from bank deposits to guest checks is possible. | | | | | | | | |
| 15. Personnel operating registers do not have access to keys which permit a display/printing of proprietary management information. | | | | | | | | |
| 16. Personnel who operate registers are held responsible for beginning cash banks. | | | | | | | | |
| 17. Each cashier has a separate register/cash drawer, if possible. | | | | | | | | |
| 18. If necessary, systems to identify responsibility for guest checks (server or cashier) are in place. | | | | | | | | |
| 19. Cash register transactions are printed on guest checks. | | | | | | | | |

| Factor | In Use (✓) | Corrective Action Required | | | | | Assigned To | Compliance Date |
|---|---|---|---|---|---|---|---|---|
| | | Develop | | Closer Supervision | Training Needed | Other (Describe) | | |
| | | Procedure | Policy | | | | | |
| 20. All guest checks must be approved by management before being accepted. | | | | | | | | |
| 21. Proper identification is required from all guests who desire to pay by check. | | | | | | | | |
| 22. Checks can only be written for the amount of purchases. | | | | | | | | |
| 23. Post-dated and two-party checks are not accepted. | | | | | | | | |
| 24. When credit cards are accepted, authorization procedures from the issuing institution are consistently followed. | | | | | | | | |
| 25. Credit card charges in excess of purchase amounts are not accepted. | | | | | | | | |
| 26. If pre-check registers are available, sales information from the machine(s) is checked with both guest check totals and cash register ring-ups. | | | | | | | | |

166

| Factor | In Use (√) | Corrective Action Required | | | | | Assigned To | Compliance Date |
|---|---|---|---|---|---|---|---|---|
| | | Develop | | Closer Supervision | Training Needed | Other (Describe) | | |
| | | Procedure | Policy | | | | | |
| 27. "Shoppers" are routinely used to help assure that all sales collection procedures are in constant use. | | | | | | | | |
| 28. Surprise cash register audits, including the counting of money in the drawer, are made on a random basis. | | | | | | | | |
| 29. When practical, the property participates in the services of a check acceptance company. | | | | | | | | |

167

# 37. Electronic Data Machine (Cash Register)

| Factor | Not Applicable | Is Being Done | Must Begin to Do |
|---|---|---|---|
| 1. The cash register drawer should be closed when the machine is not in use. | | | |
| 2. Where applicable, guest checks should be rung separately. | | | |
| 3. Tipped employees should not leave tip jars near the cash register. | | | |
| 4. Bills over $20.00 should be placed under the cash tray. | | | |
| 5. Bills collected from guests should remain on the register shelf until the transaction is settled. | | | |
| 6. Only the register operator—and management, of course—should have access to the register. | | | |
| 7. The correct department key must be depressed to record the type of transaction being rung on the machine. | | | |
| 8. Either separate cash registers or separate cash drawers should be used when more than one employee rings up sales on a machine. | | | |
| 9. The register user should not have access to the keys needed to read or total the machine. | | | |
| 10. Register operators should begin each shift with a new cash bank; each transaction should be rung up in the proper sequence, in the proper amount, and without "bunching" or totaling tickets. | | | |
| 11. Each employee who uses the register should have a written copy of procedures for its use. | | | |
| 12. When practical, cash register operators should call out the price of items being rung on the machine. | | | |
| 13. It should be possible to open the cash register drawer only by using the sale price or "no sale" key. | | | |

| Factor | Not Applicable | Is Being Done | Must Begin to Do |
|---|---|---|---|
| 14. Detail (sales journal) tapes should be replaced before they run out. | | | |
| 15. Registers should be emptied, unlocked, and left open when not in use. | | | |
| 16. Any type of operating problem should be reported to management as soon as possible. | | | |
| 17. Random cash register audits which include the counting of all money in the drawer should be made. | | | |
| 18. Managers, as part of their ongoing supervisory responsibilities, should closely monitor cash register operation. | | | |
| 19. Detail tapes should be studied on a random basis to uncover possible fraud. | | | |
| 20. Register operators should not be allowed to accept post-dated checks or IOUs. | | | |
| 21. Only a minimum number of managers should have cash register keys. | | | |
| 22. Register banks should be counted and exchanged each time a new register operator begins work. | | | |
| 23. Register tapes should be read and/or totaled and cleared when register operators change shifts. | | | |
| 24. All checks accepted from employees should be marked "for deposit only." | | | |
| 25. Forms should be available to record, by shift, sales from each register for the entire day. | | | |
| 26. Register balances should be reconciled with cash receipts at least once each shift. | | | |

| Factor | Not Applicable | Is Being Done | Must Begin to Do |
|---|---|---|---|
| 27. Cash income from miscellaneous sales (vending proceeds, grease, etc.) must be properly recorded in business accounts if these monies are first deposited in the register. | | | |
| 28. Cash register alarm bells or buzzer systems should not be bypassed; a noise should be heard each time the drawer is opened. | | | |
| 29. The register should be located in a place where it can be seen by the guests, employees and management. | | | |
| 30. If a register is used by a cashier who collects income, the machine should be located close to the exit. | | | |
| 31. Cash registers should be kept locked during service periods when a register operator is not available. | | | |
| 32. Audits of detail tapes should ensure continuity in transaction numbers. | | | |
| 33. Constant cash overages and shortages should be investigated. | | | |
| 34. Random and unexpected audits should be made of cash registers. | | | |
| 35. The register operator should not make any register readings. | | | |
| 36. No money should be paid out of register funds without management approval. | | | |
| 37. All employees who handle cash should be bonded. | | | |

# 38. Energy Management Procedures*

| Factor | In Use (✓) | Corrective Action Required | | | | | | Assigned To | Compliance Date |
|---|---|---|---|---|---|---|---|---|---|
| | | Develop | | Closer Supervision | Training Needed | Other (Describe) | | | |
| | | Procedure | Policy | | | | | | |
| **Section 1: General Information** | | | | | | | | | |
| 1. Schedule for preheat times for kitchen equipment is followed. | | | | | | | | | |
| 2. Food is cooked in largest possible volumes. | | | | | | | | | |
| 3. Thermostats on equipment items are adjusted to the lowest temperature that gives satisfactory results. | | | | | | | | | |
| 4. Equipment is turned off when not in use. | | | | | | | | | |
| 5. Equipment is used sequentially rather than simultaneously whenever possible. | | | | | | | | | |
| 6. Energy intensive cooking (baking, roasting, etc.) is done during non-peak demand times. | | | | | | | | | |
| 7. Cleaning schedules for equipment do not require the use of additional energy in the cleaning process (equipment is not cooled and then reheated for cleaning). | | | | | | | | | |

*Adapted from: Zaccarelli, H. and Ninemeier, J., Cost Effective Contract Food Service: An Institutional Guide, Second Edition (Winona, MN: Center for Business and Entrepreneurial Management, 1988), pp. 194–197.

| Factor | In Use (√) | Corrective Action Required | | | | | Assigned To | Compliance Date |
|---|---|---|---|---|---|---|---|---|
| | | Develop | | Closer Supervision | Training Needed | Other (Describe) | | |
| | | Procedure | Policy | | | | | |
| 8. Defective parts on equipment are replaced promptly. | | | | | | | | |
| 9. Cooking and heating units which are not needed are turned off. | | | | | | | | |
| 10. Twist-on timers or individual switches are used for food-warming infrared heat lamps. | | | | | | | | |
| 11. Timers are used for all kitchen equipment to control cooking times automatically. | | | | | | | | |
| 12. Cooking equipment is clustered together away from cooling equipment. | | | | | | | | |
| 13. Gas pressure to appliances is checked to assure that adequate pressure is available. | | | | | | | | |
| 14. A schedule is followed for equipment use. | | | | | | | | |
| 15. Equipment is not preheated before it is necessary. | | | | | | | | |
| 16. Cooking equipment is kept clean. | | | | | | | | |
| **Section 2: Energy Management When Using Oven** | | | | | | | | |
| 1. Ovens are not used for cooked-to-order production. | | | | | | | | |

| Factor | In Use (✓) | Corrective Action Required | | | | | Assigned To | Compliance Date |
|---|---|---|---|---|---|---|---|---|
| | | Develop | | Closer Supervision | Training Needed | Other (Describe) | | |
| | | Procedure | Policy | | | | | |
| 2. Ovens are turned off when not in use. | | | | | | | | |
| 3. Ovens are loaded to capacity with a two-inch clearance. | | | | | | | | |
| 4. Oven use is scheduled to take full advantage of receding heat. | | | | | | | | |
| 5. When ovens are preheated, the thermostat is set at the desired temperature. | | | | | | | | |
| 6. Oven thermostats are calibrated to assure that cooking temperature is appropriate to achieve the maximum energy efficiency. | | | | | | | | |
| 7. Oven thermometers are used to monitor oven thermostats. | | | | | | | | |
| 8. Fans on convection ovens are kept clean to provide maximum air delivery and to assure even heating throughout the oven capacity. | | | | | | | | |
| 9. The breather space below the door on the deck oven is cleaned frequently to permit proper closing of the door. | | | | | | | | |
| 10. Door hinges are kept in repair. | | | | | | | | |

| Factor | In Use (√) | Corrective Action Required | | | | | Assigned To | Compliance Date |
|---|---|---|---|---|---|---|---|---|
| | | Develop | | Closer Supervision | Training Needed | Other (Describe) | | |
| | | Procedure | Policy | | | | | |
| 11. Oven units are loaded and unloaded quickly to avoid unnecessary heat loss. | | | | | | | | |
| 12. Warm-up times are used to begin cooking food (unless this practice will cause the food to dry out or overcook). | | | | | | | | |
| 13. The cooking capacities of ovens are determined; the smallest, most efficient oven is used when possible. | | | | | | | | |
| 14. Oven doors are opened only when necessary. | | | | | | | | |
| 15. Ovens are maintained under a consistently followed preventive maintenance program. | | | | | | | | |
| 16. The correct size oven vent hood is used. | | | | | | | | |
| 17. Meat is cooked slowly at low temperatures. | | | | | | | | |
| 18. Baking and roasting tasks are scheduled so that the oven capacity can be fully utilized. | | | | | | | | |
| 19. Metal skewers are inserted lengthwise in potatoes to speed cooking. | | | | | | | | |
| 20. Microwave ovens are used when possible for reheating/reconstituting foods. | | | | | | | | |

| Factor | In Use (✓) | Develop Procedure | Develop Policy | Closer Supervision | Training Needed | Other (Describe) | Assigned To | Compliance Date |
|---|---|---|---|---|---|---|---|---|
| 21. Pans are not placed too close to the sides, back, or front of deck or convection ovens. | | | | | | | | |
| 22. Dampers on deck ovens are closed to prevent heated air from escaping out the back. | | | | | | | | |
| **Section 3: Energy Management When Using Surface Cooking Units (Griddle, Range Tops, etc.)** | | | | | | | | |
| 1. Fuel-air ratios are checked on all gas burners and adjusted to the most efficient mixture. | | | | | | | | |
| 2. Local gas utilities are consulted about the use of pilot lights. | | | | | | | | |
| 3. Foods on griddles are huddled close together whenever possible. | | | | | | | | |
| 4. Griddles are cleaned every shift after use. | | | | | | | | |
| 5. Pans are covered with lids for faster cooking. | | | | | | | | |
| 6. Foil is placed under range burners and griddles to improve efficiency and to make equipment easier to clean. | | | | | | | | |

| Factor | In Use (✓) | Corrective Action Required | | | | | Assigned To | Compliance Date |
| | | Develop | | Closer Supervision | Training Needed | Other (Describe) | | |
| | | Procedure | Policy | | | | | |
|---|---|---|---|---|---|---|---|---|
| 7. Electric range burners are always smaller than the kettle or pot placed on them. | | | | | | | | |
| 8. Kettles and pots are placed close together on range tops to decrease heat loss. | | | | | | | | |
| 9. Gas open burners are not preheated. | | | | | | | | |
| 10. Electric surfaces are turned off for a short period before the food is done (the food will continue to cook from stored energy). | | | | | | | | |
| 11. Pots and pans are carefully selected for the surface unit. | | | | | | | | |
| 12. Pans that are bent or warped are not used. | | | | | | | | |
| 13. All gas units are checked for uneven yellow flames. | | | | | | | | |
| 14. Heat is turned down when food begins to boil. | | | | | | | | |
| 15. Gas burners are not turned on until cooking is to begin. | | | | | | | | |
| 16. Only that portion of the griddle being used is heated. | | | | | | | | |

| Factor | In Use (✓) | Develop Procedure | Develop Policy | Closer Supervision | Training Needed | Other (Describe) | Assigned To | Compliance Date |
|---|---|---|---|---|---|---|---|---|
| **Section 4: Energy Management When Using Steam Cookers** | | | | | | | | |
| 1. Frozen foods are thawed in steam cookers instead of being boiled. | | | | | | | | |
| 2. Temperature is controlled to minimize the escape of steam. | | | | | | | | |
| 3. Steam cookers are cleaned often to remove lime deposits. | | | | | | | | |
| 4. Steam leaks are identified and corrected. | | | | | | | | |
| 5. Only the amount of water required to produce steam is used. | | | | | | | | |
| 6. Cooking is reduced to a simmer as soon as the steam point is reached; a pan with a tight-fitting cover is used. | | | | | | | | |
| **Section 5: Energy Management When Using Fryers** | | | | | | | | |
| 1. Baskets are not overloaded. | | | | | | | | |
| 2. Carbon buildup is checked weekly. | | | | | | | | |

| Factor | In Use (✓) | Corrective Action Required | | | | | | Assigned To | Compliance Date |
|---|---|---|---|---|---|---|---|---|---|
| | | Develop | | Closer Supervision | Training Needed | Other (Describe) | | | |
| | | Procedure | Policy | | | | | | |
| 3. Temperature of cooking oil is checked with an accurate thermometer. | | | | | | | | | |
| 4. Fryers are only preheated 7 to 15 minutes and only to 325°F to 350°F (162°C to 176°C). | | | | | | | | | |
| 5. The fryer is maintained at 200°F (94°C) during breaks in production. | | | | | | | | | |
| 6. Fat levels are maintained at the proper depth (the manufacturers's instructions are followed). | | | | | | | | | |
| **Section 6: Energy Management When Using Refrigeration and Storage Equipment** | | | | | | | | | |
| 1. Frozen food is thawed in the refrigerator. | | | | | | | | | |
| 2. Fan and condenser cleaning and compressor checks are done as part of an ongoing, regular maintenance program. | | | | | | | | | |
| 3. All door gaskets and seals are kept in good condition. | | | | | | | | | |
| 4. Doors of ice-maker storage bins are closed after each use. | | | | | | | | | |

| Factor | In Use (✓) | Develop Procedure | Develop Policy | Closer Supervision | Training Needed | Other (Describe) | Assigned To | Compliance Date |
|---|---|---|---|---|---|---|---|---|
| 5. Times when refrigerator and freezer doors are opened are scheduled. | | | | | | | | |
| 6. All food items stored in the refrigerator are covered. | | | | | | | | |
| 7. Items are not stored in front of coils in a way that restricts air flow. | | | | | | | | |
| 8. Frequently used items are placed near the front of the refrigeration unit. | | | | | | | | |
| 9. Doors are closed immediately after items have been removed from the unit. | | | | | | | | |
| 10. Coolers are not used to store individual portions of products which require opening the door every time a portion is needed. | | | | | | | | |
| 11. Lights in walk-in units are turned off when not needed. | | | | | | | | |
| 12. Refrigerators are checked for short cycling and loss of temperature. | | | | | | | | |
| 13. Compressor coils are kept free of dust. | | | | | | | | |

*Column group header: "Corrective Action Required" spans Develop (Procedure, Policy), Closer Supervision, Training Needed, Other (Describe).*

| Factor | In Use (√) | Corrective Action Required | | | | | Assigned To | Compliance Date |
|---|---|---|---|---|---|---|---|---|
| | | Develop | | Closer Supervision | Training Needed | Other (Describe) | | |
| | | Procedure | Policy | | | | | |
| 14. Compressors are placed in cool areas rather than near heating units. | | | | | | | | |
| 15. Freezer fans are cleaned periodically and compressors are checked regularly. | | | | | | | | |
| 16. Refrigeration and freezer space is consolidated where possible. | | | | | | | | |
| 17. Receiving is expedited to assure prompt refrigeration of frozen and perishable foods. | | | | | | | | |
| 18. Freezers are defrosted frequently. | | | | | | | | |
| **Section 7: Energy Management When Using Dishwashing Equipment** | | | | | | | | |
| 1. Reduce the amount of hot water used by monitoring the amount wasted. | | | | | | | | |
| 2. Use the lowest temperature appropriate to the use intended. | | | | | | | | |
| 3. Keep distribution runs as short as possible; hot water boosters should be located within 48 inches of dishwasher to avoid heat loss in the run. | | | | | | | | |

| Factor | In Use (✓) | Develop Procedure | Develop Policy | Closer Supervision | Training Needed | Other (Describe) | Assigned To | Compliance Date |
|---|---|---|---|---|---|---|---|---|
| | | | | | | Corrective Action Required | | |
| 4. Use spring-operated valves on the hand levers and food pedals to save water. | | | | | | | | |
| 5. Keep booster heater off until it is needed. | | | | | | | | |
| 6. Turn off dishwasher after use. | | | | | | | | |
| 7. Regularly check the rinse water temperature. | | | | | | | | |
| 8. Regularly remove lime deposits from spray nozzles and tanks. | | | | | | | | |
| 9. Check pumps monthly for water leakage. | | | | | | | | |
| 10. Check feed and drain valves weekly for water leakage. | | | | | | | | |
| 11. Schedule dishwasher for efficient use; use the dish machine at specified times during the day rather than running short loads all day long; wash only full racks of dishes whenever possible. | | | | | | | | |
| 12. Keep the power dryer to minimum use. | | | | | | | | |
| 13. Consider wetting agents versus power drying. | | | | | | | | |

| Factor | In Use (√) | Corrective Action Required | | | | | Assigned To | Compliance Date |
|---|---|---|---|---|---|---|---|---|
| | | Develop | | Closer Supervision | Training Needed | Other (Describe) | | |
| | | Policy | Procedure | | | | | |
| 14. Dishwasher exhaust should operate only when dishwasher is in use. | | | | | | | | |
| 15. Consider using sanitizing solutions that allow for lower temperatures; e.g., cold chemical ware washing systems. | | | | | | | | |
| 16. Check local sanitary codes to ensure that water is supplied at the lowest possible temperature. | | | | | | | | |
| 17. Install pressure regulators if not already present. | | | | | | | | |
| 18. Replace water jets that allow too much water to flow through the dishwasher. | | | | | | | | |
| 19. Insulate heating pipes and hot water lines. | | | | | | | | |
| 20. Stop leakage; check pipes and faucets. | | | | | | | | |
| 21. Caution personnel to avoid letting faucets run unnecessarily. | | | | | | | | |
| 22. Keep heater coils free from lime accumulation. | | | | | | | | |
| 23. When the main dish washing is over, turn off the equipment heat boosters and accumulate dishes until the next rush period. | | | | | | | | |

| Factor | In Use (✓) | Corrective Action Required | | | | | Assigned To | Compliance Date |
|---|---|---|---|---|---|---|---|---|
| | | Develop | | Closer Supervision | Training Needed | Other (Describe) | | |
| | | Procedure | Policy | | | | | |
| 24. Obtain water pressure for the hot water line to dishwasher to reduce wasted hot water; set regulator to the operating pressure required by the machine; make sure power rinse is turning off automatically when tray has gone through the machine. | | | | | | | | |
| **Section 8: Hot Water Consumption Procedures** | | | | | | | | |
| 1. Use hot water only when cold water will not do the job. | | | | | | | | |
| 2. Do not leave faucets running. | | | | | | | | |
| 3. In pot-washing area, fill sinks for washing utensils instead of using continuously running water. | | | | | | | | |
| 4. Repair leaky faucets. | | | | | | | | |
| 5. Use flow restrictions in faucets. | | | | | | | | |
| 6. Use hot tap water for cooking when possible. | | | | | | | | |
| 7. Use water heater only to heat water to required temperature. | | | | | | | | |

183

| Factor | In Use (✓) | Corrective Action Required | | | | | | Assigned To | Compliance Date |
|---|---|---|---|---|---|---|---|---|---|
| | | Develop | | Closer Supervision | Training Needed | Other (Describe) | | | |
| | | Procedure | Policy | | | | | | |
| 8. Check insulation on hot water pipes; repair/replace as necessary. | | | | | | | | | |
| 9. Check steam water heater for steam flow through steam trap. | | | | | | | | | |
| 10. Drain and flush hot water tanks twice a year. | | | | | | | | | |
| **Section 9: Energy Management Concerns with Heating, Ventilation, and Air Conditioning (HVAC) Systems** | | | | | | | | | |
| 1. Turn systems off in unoccupied spaces. | | | | | | | | | |
| 2. Set room temperature controls to 78°F in summer and 68°F in winter. | | | | | | | | | |
| 3. Turn off supply/exhaust fans when they are not needed. | | | | | | | | | |
| 4. Clean/replace filters on appropriate schedule. | | | | | | | | | |
| 5. Clean heating, cooling, and condensing coils on appropriate schedule. | | | | | | | | | |
| 6. Use outside air when possible to reduce cooling system loads. | | | | | | | | | |

184

| Factor | In Use (✓) | Corrective Action Required | | | | | Assigned To | Compliance Date |
|---|---|---|---|---|---|---|---|---|
| | | Develop | | Closer Supervision | Training Needed | Other (Describe) | | |
| | | Procedure | Policy | | | | | |
| **Section 10: Energy Management Concerns with Lighting Systems** | | | | | | | | |
| 1. Turn off lights when not needed. | | | | | | | | |
| 2. Develop a lighting plan that emphasizes minimum required lighting levels. | | | | | | | | |
| 3. Replace lamps with smaller units and remove excess lamps in accordance with the lighting plan. | | | | | | | | |
| 4. Clean and wash walls, ceilings, and floors (light reflecting surfaces require less artificial lighting). | | | | | | | | |
| 5. Use light colors for interior surfaces when possible. | | | | | | | | |
| 6. Use fluorescent lamps when possible. | | | | | | | | |
| 7. Clean light fixtures at appropriate intervals. | | | | | | | | |
| 8. When possible, and if necessary, reposition lamp fixtures to areas where employees perform most work activities. | | | | | | | | |
| 9. Schedule cleaning of areas for daylight hours when possible. | | | | | | | | |

## 39. Bartender Control Procedures

| Factor | In Use (✓) | Corrective Action Required | | | | | Assigned To | Compliance Date |
|---|---|---|---|---|---|---|---|---|
| | | Develop | | Closer Supervision | Training Needed | Other (Describe) | | |
| | | Procedure | Policy | | | | | |
| 1. Bartenders are required to consistently follow standard recipes as drinks are prepared. | | | | | | | | |
| 2. Bartenders are required to consistently use applicable electronic data machine (cash register) operating procedures. | | | | | | | | |
| 3. "Shoppers" are routinely used to confirm bartender compliance with all applicable policies and procedures. | | | | | | | | |
| 4. When practical, bartender and beverage server staff are placed on rotating work schedule. | | | | | | | | |
| 5. Bartenders are not permitted to "comp" drinks to guests. | | | | | | | | |
| 6. Tip jars are located away from the cash register. | | | | | | | | |
| 7. When practical, guest checks are completed by bartenders before drinks are prepared/served. | | | | | | | | |

| Factor | In Use (√) | Develop Procedure | Develop Policy | Closer Supervision | Training Needed | Other (Describe) | Assigned To | Compliance Date |
|---|---|---|---|---|---|---|---|---|
| | | | | Corrective Action Required | | | | |
| 8. Bartenders do not have access to keys required to generate sales data from the cash register. | | | | | | | | |
| 9. Bartenders are held responsible for cash in opening banks during their shift. | | | | | | | | |
| 10. Bartenders are held responsible for par levels of alcoholic beverage inventory. | | | | | | | | |
| 11. Bartenders must consistently follow all required check and/or credit card acceptance procedures. | | | | | | | | |
| 12. Bartenders are required to pre-prepare garnishes, mixes and other items according to quantities determined by management. | | | | | | | | |
| 13. Bartenders are not permitted access to liquor storage areas. | | | | | | | | |
| 14. Behind-bar storage areas are kept locked when the bar is not open. | | | | | | | | |
| 15. Issues of beverages to the bar are made on the basis of empty bottles. | | | | | | | | |

| Factor | In Use (✓) | Corrective Action Required | | | | | Assigned To | Compliance Date |
|---|---|---|---|---|---|---|---|---|
| | | Develop | | Closer Supervision | Training Needed | Other (Describe) | | |
| | | Procedure | Policy | | | | | |
| 16. Bartenders are not permitted to drink or to accept drinks from guests while working. | | | | | | | | |
| 17. Bartenders are not permitted to give drinks to other employees. | | | | | | | | |
| 18. All returned drinks should be shown to management before discarding. | | | | | | | | |
| 19. Proper portion control tools must be used at all times. | | | | | | | | |
| 20. Policies regarding employee visiting/drinking at the bar before, after, and during work are strictly enforced. | | | | | | | | |
| 21. Only management personnel determine drink selling prices. | | | | | | | | |
| 22. Management procedures to help assure sales income control practices are consistently followed. | | | | | | | | |
| 23. Bartender staff participates in the property's ongoing guest relations program. | | | | | | | | |

| Factor | In Use (✓) | Corrective Action Required | | | | | | Assigned To | Compliance Date |
|---|---|---|---|---|---|---|---|---|---|
| | | Develop | | Closer Supervision | Training Needed | Other (Describe) | | | |
| | | Procedure | Policy | | | | | | |
| 24. Bartender staff does not routinely meet with sales representatives of alcoholic beverage distributing companies. | | | | | | | | | |
| 25. All bottles are marked with the property's identifying logo before being issued to the bar. | | | | | | | | | |
| 26. Bartenders are trained in the property's requirements regarding fire, bomb threat, robbery, and related procedures. | | | | | | | | | |
| 27. Bartenders consistently follow the property's requirements relating to the proper and legal service of alcoholic beverages. | | | | | | | | | |

# Part VII | Property Evaluation Procedures

# 40. Operational Review (Institutional Food Services)

| Factor | C | TC | NC | NA | Comments |
|---|---|---|---|---|---|
| **Section 1: Records**<br><br>*General Policies and Documentation*<br><br>1. Updated copy of the company's operating procedures. | | | | | |
| 2. Current copy of applicable diet manuals | | | | | |
| 3. Current Food Handler's Certificate for each employee. | | | | | |
| 4. The company's policy and procedure manual contains information about: | | | | | |
| a. Table of contents w/page numbers. | | | | | |
| b. Facility objectives. | | | | | |
| c. Current facility/department organization chart. | | | | | |
| d. General emergency plan (may be in separate folder). | | | | | |
| e. Emergency feeding plan (may be in separate folder w/manual). | | | | | |
| f. Active and preventative maintenance plan. | | | | | |
| g. Procedure for food delivery (including loading, pick-up, and snacks). | | | | | |
| h. Equipment operating and cleaning procedures. (Are they posted near equipment in all areas?) | | | | | |

C = Compliance; TC = Toward Compliance; NC = Noncompliance; NA = Not Applicable.

*From: Zaccarelli, H. and Ninemeier, J., *Cost Effective Contract Food Service: An Institutional Guide*, Second Edition (Winona, MN: Center for Business and Entrepreneurial Management, 1988), pp. 131-137.

| Factor | C | TC | NC | NA | Comments |
|---|---|---|---|---|---|
| i. Method of insuring that each client receives correct diet. | | | | | |
| j. Alterations in diet schedules for holding trays, late trays, isolations, etc. | | | | | |
| k. Procedure for direct care and food services responsibilities in the dining room during meal service. | | | | | |
| l. Procedure for food delivery to clients in isolation. | | | | | |
| m. Snack policy and procedure for serving them. | | | | | |
| n. Current job description for each position. | | | | | |
| o. All procedures approved by the administration. | | | | | |
| p. All procedures relating to other departments coordinated w/copies of procedures available in that department. | | | | | |
| q. Procedures for receiving diet orders, reviews by dietitian. | | | | | |
| r. Procedures for coordinating menu changes with dietitian. | | | | | |
| s. Procedures for interchanging information on food ordering with dietitian. | | | | | |
| t. Procedures for scheduling of employee days off and on the job. | | | | | |
| u. Procedures for scheduling employee placement in units. | | | | | |
| 5. In-service training including: | | | | | |

C = Compliance; TC = Toward Compliance; NC = Noncompliance; NA = Not Applicable.

| Factor | C | TC | NC | NA | Comments |
|---|---|---|---|---|---|
| a. Periodic sessions, dates. | | | | | |
| b. Outline of content (content format). | | | | | |
| c. Comprehensive curriculum. | | | | | |
| d. Personal hygiene. | | | | | |
| e. Proper handling and preparation of food (sanitation). | | | | | |
| f. Proper serving of food (portion control). | | | | | |
| g. Nutritional needs of clients. | | | | | |
| h. Serving modified diets. | | | | | |
| i. Proper cleaning and operation of equipment. | | | | | |
| j. Record of attendance with employee signature. | | | | | |
| k. Make-up procedures available and followed. | | | | | |
| l. Job orientation documentation. | | | | | |
| 6. Records of food acceptance studies. | | | | | |
| 7. Menus as served for the past 30 days. | | | | | |
| 8. Snack menu. | | | | | |
| 9. Records of bacteriological test results and (if available) health inspection reports: <br><br> a. Performed and recorded on food utensils and various pieces of equipment. | | | | | |

C = Compliance; TC = Toward Compliance; NC = Noncompliance; NA = Not Applicable.

| Factor | C | TC | NC | NA | Comments |
|---|---|---|---|---|---|
| b. Performed monthly and recorded on ice cream and milk, to include butterfat percentage. | | | | | |
| c. Sent to Director of Nutrition and Food Service. | | | | | |
| 10. Current client diet orders on file and outdated orders removed from file. | | | | | |
| 11. Staffing in accordance with prescribed staffing ratios. | | | | | |
| 12. Methods of assignment for client workers are in accordance with policies and procedures of the programs. | | | | | |
| 13. Health policies and procedures for client workers are the same as food service employees. | | | | | |
| 14. Diet orders correspond to current doctor's orders (check a minimum of 20). | | | | | |
| 15. Other (specify): _____ _____ | | | | | |
| **Section 2: Meal Service Observation** *Location:* _____ 1. Menu. a. Available in serving area. | | | | | |
| b. Menu for every modified diet. | | | | | |
| c. Corresponds to food served. | | | | | |

C = Compliance; TC = Toward Compliance; NC = Noncompliance; NA = Not Applicable.

| Factor | C | TC | NC | NA | Comments |
|---|---|---|---|---|---|
| d. Substitutions are of equal value. | | | | | |
| e. Used as reference during serving. | | | | | |
| f. Substitutions documented in serving area. | | | | | |
| 2. Meal service.<br><br>  a. On schedule. | | | | | |
| b. Acceptable intervals between meals. | | | | | |
| c. Serving area clean and well lighted. | | | | | |
| d. Food on serving line separated from clients. | | | | | |
| 3. Temperature of food.<br><br>  a. Hot food is 140°F.<br>  Food Item          Temperature<br>  _____   _____<br>  _____   _____<br>  _____   _____<br>  _____   _____<br>  _____   _____<br>  _____   _____ | | | | | |
| b. Cold food is 45°F or below.<br>  Food Item          Temperature<br>  _____   _____<br>  _____   _____<br>  _____   _____<br>  _____   _____<br>  _____   _____<br>  _____   _____ | | | | | |
| 4. Accurate portion control. | | | | | |

C = Compliance; TC = Toward Compliance; NC = Noncompliance; NA = Not Applicable.

| Factor | C | TC | NC | NA | Comments |
|---|---|---|---|---|---|
| a. Proper serving utensils. | | | | | |
| b. Proper serving size when utensils not used. | | | | | |
| 5. Sanitary dispensing of ice. | | | | | |
| 6. Sanitary serving of beverages. | | | | | |
| 7. Proper use of plastic hand guards. | | | | | |
| 8. Sanitary procedures utilized in serving of food, seconds served in disposables or clean tray, plate, etc. | | | | | |
| 9. Diet cards or diet rosters used. | | | | | |
| 10. Accurate serving of modified diets. a. Number observed: | | | | | |
| b. Number correct: | | | | | |
| 11. Are there sufficient food service personnel to serve all food? | | | | | |
| 12. Sanitary methods of handling dishes and flatware. a. Dirty dish area separate from clean dish area. | | | | | |
| b. Disposal clean and odor free. | | | | | |
| c. Machine clean and delimed. | | | | | |
| d. Dishmachine temperatures recorded. | | | | | |

C = Compliance; TC = Toward Compliance; NC = Noncompliance; NA = Not Applicable.

| Factor | C | TC | NC | NA | Comments |
|---|---|---|---|---|---|
| e. Detergent and soap storage clean and neat and separate from food items. | | | | | |
| f. Cracked and chipped dishes properly disposed of. | | | | | |
| g. Soiled dishes scraped before washing. | | | | | |
| h. Dishwashing racks are not overloaded. | | | | | |
| i. Dishwashing racks clean and in good condition. | | | | | |
| j. Dishroom cross contamination eliminated. | | | | | |
| k. Dishes are dried without using a dish towel. | | | | | |
| l. Knives, forks, and spoons washed in dishwasher with tines, blades and bowls up and transferred to a sterilized container with handles up. | | | | | |
| m. Adequate cylinders for above items. | | | | | |
| n. Knives, forks, and spoons, and special eating devices washed and rinsed like all dishes in dishmachine. | | | | | |
| o. Dishes stored in a dust-, rodent-, insect-free place. | | | | | |
| p. Food trays stored bottom side up or in tray rack so they will drain. | | | | | |
| 13. Refrigerators and coolers. | | | | | |
| a. Interior of refrigerator in unit kitchen clean and odor free. | | | | | |

C = Compliance; TC = Toward Compliance; NC = Noncompliance; NA = Not Applicable.

| Factor | C | TC | NC | NA | Comments |
|---|---|---|---|---|---|
| b. All food in refrigerator labeled and dated. | | | | | |
| c. Thermometer in each refrigerator. | | | | | |
| d. Refrigerator temperature 40°F. | | | | | |
| e. The gaskets and door area on milk coolers are clean and free from mildew stain. | | | | | |
| f. Refrigerator hinges and latches clean. | | | | | |
| 14. Waste handling. | | | | | |
| a. Garbage properly covered in dining and serving areas. | | | | | |
| b. Adequate separation between serving area and garbage and trash. | | | | | |
| c. Pest control effective. | | | | | |
| d. Waste kept in leakproof, nonabsorbent containers. | | | | | |
| 15. Dining area. | | | | | |
| a. Dining area congenial, attractive. | | | | | |
| b. Tables and chairs in dining area washed and sanitized after each meal service. | | | | | |
| c. Dining area well ventilated and odor free. | | | | | |
| d. Dining area clean. | | | | | |
| 16. Adequate hand washing facilities for staff (and clients, if applicable). | | | | | |

C = Compliance; TC = Toward Compliance; NC = Noncompliance; NA = Not Applicable.

| Factor | C | TC | NC | NA | Comments |
|---|---|---|---|---|---|
| 17. Safety. | | | | | |
| a. All electrical cords and connections in good repair. | | | | | |
| b. A fire extinguisher present in strategic locations. | | | | | |
| 18. Occupational therapy's relationship to food service. | | | | | |
| a. Special utensils provided for clients needing them. | | | | | |
| b. Appropriate utensils available for feeding (knives, forks, spoons). | | | | | |
| c. Dining rooms adequately supervised and staffed for the direction of self-help dining procedures. | | | | | |
| d. Clients provided with systematic training to develop appropriate eating skills, utilizing adaptive equipment where necessary. | | | | | |
| e. Direct care staff trained to utilize proper techniques in feeding clients. | | | | | |
| f. Clients eat in upright position. | | | | | |
| g. Clients' eating diets consistent with developmental needs. | | | | | |
| h. Occupational therapy department evaluates each client concerning feeding skills. | | | | | |
| 19. Family style meal service.<br><br>Location:_____ | | | | | |

C = Compliance; TC = Toward Compliance; NC = Noncompliance; NA = Not Applicable.

| Factor | C | TC | NC | NA | Comments |
|---|---|---|---|---|---|
| a. Involvement of clients. | | | | | |
| b. Clients receive correct modified diet (including direct care staff adequately trained in diets). | | | | | |
| c. Adequate number of direct care staff for supervising clients. | | | | | |
| d. Clients provided with training to develop self help skills if appropriate (meal planning, cooking, purchasing, etc.). | | | | | |
| 20. Others (specify): | | | | | |
| **Section 3: Central Kitchen** 1. Work area—sanitation. a. Floor in good repair and clean. | | | | | |
| b. Floors have sufficient drains in good condition and clean. | | | | | |
| c. Walls and ceilings clean and in good repair. | | | | | |
| d. Exposed pipes properly insulated. | | | | | |
| e. Doors and windows screened. | | | | | |
| f. Outside doors self-closing. | | | | | |
| g. Mats and baseboards clean. | | | | | |
| h. Food preparation areas well lighted. | | | | | |
| i. All rooms adequately ventilated. | | | | | |

C = Compliance; TC = Toward Compliance; NC = Noncompliance; NA = Not Applicable.

| Factor | C | TC | NC | NA | Comments |
|---|---|---|---|---|---|
| j.  Entrance ways clean and orderly. | | | | | |
| k. Overhead hoods in correct position and installed where necessary. | | | | | |
| l. Hoods, ventilators and filters, and surrounding areas free of grease and dirt. | | | | | |
| m. All hidden spots including corners and behind equipment clean. | | | | | |
| n. General appearance of the department indicates frequent cleaning of rooms and equipment. | | | | | |
| o. Handwashing facilities convenient with soap available and paper towels or dryer. | | | | | |
| p. Pest control procedures effective. | | | | | |
| q. Milk and ice cream cabinets regularly defrosted and cleaned. | | | | | |
| r. Light bulbs and fixtures clean. | | | | | |
| s. All electrical cords and connections in good repair. | | | | | |
| t. Casters and wheels on carts clean and well lubricated. | | | | | |
| u. Sanitary method of ice dispensing. | | | | | |
| v. Burners and area beneath burners on stoves and grills are clean. | | | | | |
| w. Trash containers leakproof, nonabsorbent, and covered. | | | | | |

C = Compliance; TC = Toward Compliance; NC = Noncompliance; NA = Not Applicable.

| Factor | C | TC | NC | NA | Comments |
|---|---|---|---|---|---|
| 2. Work area—safety.<br><br>a. Fire extinguishers located in strategic locations and in sufficient quantity. | | | | | |
| b. In slick floor areas, mats or other means used to prevent slippage. | | | | | |
| 3. Kitchen equipment and utensils.<br><br>a. Utensils and equipment in good repair—free of breaks, open seams, cracks, and chips. | | | | | |
| b. Utensils and food contact surfaces of equipment clean to sight and touch. | | | | | |
| c. Utensils, kitchenware, and nonstationary equipment stored in a clean dry place at sufficient height from floor and protected from dust, flies, and other contamination. | | | | | |
| d. Posted instructions for the operating and cleaning of all equipment. | | | | | |
| 4. Adequate facilities for maintaining food at proper serving temperatures. | | | | | |
| 5. Mop storage.<br><br>a. Mop storage area well organized and clean. | | | | | |
| b. Mops and brooms correctly stored (head down). | | | | | |
| c. Mops and brushes clean and in good repair. | | | | | |

C = Compliance; TC = Toward Compliance; NC = Noncompliance; NA = Not Applicable.

| Factor | C | TC | NC | NA | Comments |
|---|---|---|---|---|---|
| 6. Other storage areas. | | | | | |
|    a. Stored materials arranged in an orderly manner in a clean area. | | | | | |
|    b. Stored materials the proper distance from the floor. | | | | | |
| 7. Dishwashing. | | | | | |
|    a. Disposal clean and odor free. | | | | | |
|    b. Machine clean and limed. | | | | | |
|    c. Detergent and soap storage clean and neat and separate from food items. | | | | | |
|    d. Dishmachine temperatures recorded and correct. | | | | | |
|    e. Cracked and chipped dishes properly disposed of. | | | | | |
|    f. Soiled dishes scraped before washing. | | | | | |
|    g. Dishwashing racks clean and in good condition. | | | | | |
|    h. Dishwashing racks are not overloaded. | | | | | |
|    i. Dishroom cross contamination eliminated. | | | | | |
|    j. Dishes air dried without using a dish towel. | | | | | |
|    k. Knives, forks, and spoons washed in dishwasher with tines, blades, and bowls up and transferred to a sterilized container with handles up. | | | | | |

C = Compliance; TC = Toward Compliance; NC = Noncompliance; NA = Not Applicable.

| Factor | C | TC | NC | NA | Comments |
|---|---|---|---|---|---|
| l. Adequate cylinders to do above items. | | | | | |
| m. Knives, forks, and spoons and special devices washed and rinsed like all dishes in dishmachine. | | | | | |
| n. Dishes stored in a dust-, rodent-, insect-free place. | | | | | |
| o. Food trays stored bottom side up or in tray rack so they will drain. | | | | | |
| p. Waste kept in leakproof, nonabsorbent containers with close fitting covers and disposed of daily. | | | | | |
| 8. Pot washing. | | | | | |
| a. Sanitary procedures used in pot washing. | | | | | |
| b. Correct temperatures reached. | | | | | |
| 9. Food supplies—ingredient room. | | | | | |
| a. Storeroom ventilated and at an acceptable temperature. | | | | | |
| b. Entire storeroom kept clean and neat. | | | | | |
| c. All supplies stored properly above floor level. | | | | | |
| d. Old supplies are used first. | | | | | |
| e. All drums and other bulk containers are covered and labeled. | | | | | |
| f. Scoops stored properly. | | | | | |
| g. Cleaning compounds stored separately. | | | | | |

C = Compliance; TC = Toward Compliance; NC = Noncompliance; NA = Not Applicable.

| Factor | C | TC | NC | NA | Comments |
|---|---|---|---|---|---|
| h.  Work tables clean and orderly. | | | | | |
| i.  All canned goods free of dents and bulges. | | | | | |
| j.  Shelves and platforms clean. | | | | | |
| 10.  Personnel. | | | | | |
| a. Food service employees properly dressed. | | | | | |
| b. Observance of infectious and/or open skin lesions. | | | | | |
| c.  Employees smoking only in designated area. | | | | | |
| d. Dressing rooms and lockers kept clean. | | | | | |
| 11.  Refrigeration. | | | | | |
| a. All foods properly stored in refrigerator and freezers; labeled, covered and dated. | | | | | |
| b. Foods stored acceptable distance from floor. | | | | | |
| c.  Walk-in refrigerators open from inside. | | | | | |
| d. Interior of refrigerators and freezers clean. | | | | | |
| e. Thermometers in each refrigerator and freezer. | | | | | |
| f.  Frozen foods stored at 0°F or below. | | | | | |
| g. Fresh meat, poultry, fish and dairy products stored at 33°F to 40°F. | | | | | |

C = Compliance; TC = Toward Compliance; NC = Noncompliance; NA = Not Applicable.

| Factor | C | TC | NC | NA | Comments |
|---|---|---|---|---|---|
| 12. Food handling. | | | | | |
|    a. Plastic gloves used if mixing is done with hands. | | | | | |
|    b. Food handled in a sanitary and safe manner. | | | | | |
|    c. Work areas neat—with no spillage on floor. | | | | | |
|    d. Frozen food thawed appropriately. | | | | | |
| 13. Modified diet preparation. | | | | | |
|    a. Modified diet menus and guidelines are followed. | | | | | |
|    b. Proper amount(s) to meet facility needs is/are prepared. | | | | | |
| 14. Other (specify): _____ _____ | | | | | |
| **Section 4: Special Needs of Clients** | | | | | |
| 1. Snacks available for children and adolescents and other clients according to their needs. | | | | | |
| 2. Special adjustment where appropriate on menu choices for the needs of children, adolescents, and geriatrics. | | | | | |
| 3. Children and adolescent units—all refrigerators and freezers are capable of being opened from the inside. | | | | | |
| 4. Other (specify): _____ _____ | | | | | |

C = Compliance; TC = Toward Compliance; NC = Noncompliance; NA = Not Applicable.

| Factor | C | TC | NC | NA | Comments |
|---|---|---|---|---|---|
| **Section 5: Nutrition Documentation**<br><br>1. Nutrition/dietary services records.<br><br>   a. Diet histories completed within one week of admission. | | | | | |
|    b. Copies of diet histories and assessments are in correct files. | | | | | |
| 2. Effective filing procedures in use. | | | | | |
| 3. Records of all clients on modified diets are available. | | | | | |
| 4. Reports of meal observations are available. | | | | | |
| 5. Records of all clients on modified diets are available. | | | | | |
| 6. Necessary duplicates of nutritional documentation in clients' records. | | | | | |
| 7. Documentation in client records; select as many records as possible (a minimum of 20) to include at least one record from each unit of the facility. Check for:<br><br>   a. Nutritional assessment/evaluation. | | | | | |
|    &bull; Comprehensive. | | | | | |
|    &bull; Accuracy of data. | | | | | |
|    &bull; Evaluator's judgment of objective and subjective data. | | | | | |
|    b. Nutritional objective or goal/approaches or strategies stated if problem revealed in staffings. | | | | | |

C = Compliance; TC = Toward Compliance; NC = Noncompliance; NA = Not Applicable.

| Factor | C | TC | NC | NA | Comments |
|---|---|---|---|---|---|
| c. Quality of goals or objectives/approaches or strategies. | | | | | |
| • Comprehensive. | | | | | |
| • Realistic. | | | | | |
| d. Mental health. | | | | | |
| • Assessment/evaluation on all clients. | | | | | |
| e. Mental retardation. | | | | | |
| • Yearly staffing summary by dietitian (includes comprehensive, accuracy of data, evaluator's judgment of objective and subjective data). | | | | | |
| f. Progress noted/monitoring. | | | | | |
| • Relate to original goal. | | | | | |
| • Progress noted according to frequency stated in plan. | | | | | |
| 8. Policy and procedure manual information includes: | | | | | |
| a. Job description. | | | | | |
| b. Organization plan. | | | | | |
| c. Procedures for taking diet histories. | | | | | |
| d. Procedures for total nutritional care to include, but not limited to: | | | | | |
| • Assessments/evaluations (significant information from diet history included). | | | | | |

C = Compliance; TC = Toward Compliance; NC = Noncompliance; NA = Not Applicable.

| Factor | C | TC | NC | NA | Comments |
|---|---|---|---|---|---|
| • Follow-up to assessments/evaluations as appropriate. | | | | | |
| • Procedures for incorporating all necessary information into client's records. | | | | | |
| • Client and/or family counseling. | | | | | |
| • Procedures for attending staff meetings. | | | | | |
| • Procedures for referrals/ consultations. | | | | | |
| • Procedures for receiving significant weight changes of clients coordinated with nursing service. | | | | | |
| • Specific procedures for coordinating menu changes with food service department. | | | | | |
| • Receiving and renewing diet orders. | | | | | |
| e. Coordinating menu changes with food service department. | | | | | |
| f. Procedures for interchanging information on food ordering with food service manager. | | | | | |
| 9. Other related documentation. | | | | | |
| a. Dietary consumption of the client accurately documented. | | | | | |
| b. Height and weight data available. | | | | | |
| c. Other: _____ | | | | | |

C = Compliance; TC = Toward Compliance; NC = Noncompliance; NA = Not Applicable.

| Factor | C | TC | NC | NA | Comments |
|---|---|---|---|---|---|
| 10. Other (specify): _____ _____ | | | | | |

C = Compliance; TC = Toward Compliance; NC = Noncompliance; NA = Not Applicable.

# 41. Shopper's Report (Commercial Food Services)

Name of Property: _____

Date of Visit: _____

| | Strongly Agree | Agree | Disagree | Strongly Disagree |
|---|---|---|---|---|
| **Reservation Request** | | | | |
| 1. Reservation telephone call answered within three rings. | | | | |
| 2. The individual who answered the phone identified himself/herself and the dining room with a pleasant voice. | | | | |
| 3. Reservation was handled courteously. | | | | |
| 4. Reservationist used your name and thanked you for the reservation. | | | | |
| Comments: _____ _____ _____ _____ _____ _____ | | | | |
| **Building Exterior** | | | | |
| 1. Adequate parking spaces available. | | | | |
| 2. Sign easily seen from a distance. | | | | |
| 3. Sign easily read, in good repair, and clean. | | | | |
| 4. Grounds free of debris and neatly maintained. | | | | |
| 5. Area surrounding dining room well landscaped and well lighted. | | | | |
| 6. Area free from loud noises and setting comfortable. | | | | |

| | Strongly Agree | Agree | Disagree | Strongly Disagree |
|---|---|---|---|---|
| 7. Music tastefully distant. | | | | |
| Comments:<br><br>_____<br>_____<br>_____<br>_____<br>_____<br>_____ | | | | |

## Arrival

| | Strongly Agree | Agree | Disagree | Strongly Disagree |
|---|---|---|---|---|
| 1. Greeted immediately upon entering dining room. | | | | |
| 2. The host/hostess asked for name and/or made a friendly comment. | | | | |
| 3. The host/hostess asked about a smoking/non-smoking table. | | | | |
| 4. Seated within a reasonable time (three minutes). | | | | |
| 5. Host/hostess attractively dressed with pleasant smile. | | | | |
| Comments:<br><br>_____<br>_____<br>_____<br>_____<br>_____ | | | | |

## Seating

| | Strongly Agree | Agree | Disagree | Strongly Disagree |
|---|---|---|---|---|
| 1. Lounge offered as an alternative if party had to wait. | | | | |
| 2. Selection of table location showed good judgment. | | | | |
| 3. Host/hostess helped seat at least one guest. | | | | |
| 4. Chair or booth comfortable and provided easy access. | | | | |

| | Strongly Agree | Agree | Disagree | Strongly Disagree |
|---|---|---|---|---|
| 5. Distribution of menus comfortable, and placement favored each guest. | | | | |
| 6. Host/hostess informed you of specials and/or menu additions. | | | | |
| 7. Host/hostess informed you of server's name. | | | | |
| 8. Host/hostess left with a pleasant message. | | | | |
| 9. Host/hostess seemed happy and felt good about having you there. | | | | |
| Comments: _____ _____ _____ _____ _____ _____ | | | | |
| **Menu** 1. Menu was clean and free from spots. | | | | |
| 2. Menu fit the theme of the dining room. | | | | |
| 3. Menu was well organized and size was physically manageable. | | | | |
| 4. Menu was clearly written and number of items was appropriate. | | | | |
| 5. Menu was easily read and descriptions were appetizing. | | | | |
| 6. Menu was a marketing tool. | | | | |
| 7. Specials were available. | | | | |
| 8. Vegetarian and children's portions were available. | | | | |

| | Strongly Agree | Agree | Disagree | Strongly Disagree |
|---|---|---|---|---|
| Comments: <br><br> _____ <br> _____ <br> _____ <br> _____ <br> _____ <br> _____ | | | | |
| **Waiting (Bus) Service** | | | | |
| 1. Bus help provided water during first contact. | | | | |
| 2. Water glasses refilled promptly. | | | | |
| 3. Dirty dishware removed from the right. | | | | |
| 4. Dirty dishware removed as soon as empty. | | | | |
| 5. Dirty ashtrays were properly removed (capped) and replaced. | | | | |
| 6. Employee appeared to enjoy job. | | | | |
| 7. Uniform clean and attractive. | | | | |
| 8. Employee clean and well groomed. | | | | |
| 9. Employee did an excellent job. | | | | |
| 10. Employee's service was uninterruptive. | | | | |
| Comments: <br><br> _____ <br> _____ <br> _____ <br> _____ <br> _____ <br> _____ | | | | |

| | Strongly Agree | Agree | Disagree | Strongly Disagree |
|---|---|---|---|---|
| **Server** | | | | |
| 1. Server made contact within three minutes after seating. | | | | |
| 2. Server introduced himself/herself and had a pleasant greeting. | | | | |
| 3. Server's hands and fingernails were clean. | | | | |
| 4. Server's uniform clean and attractive. | | | | |
| 5. Server smiled, was cordial, and created a pleasant atmosphere. | | | | |
| 6. Server was familiar with all menu items. | | | | |
| 7. Server used suggestive selling techniques. | | | | |
| 8. Server could answer all questions regarding dining room. | | | | |
| 9. Beverage items were served from the left promptly. | | | | |
| 10. Food items were served from the left promptly. | | | | |
| 11. Timing between courses was appropriate. | | | | |
| 12. Server knew which items to serve each guest. | | | | |
| 13. Server returned to table to provide additional service after main course arrived. | | | | |
| 14. It was not necessary to summon the server during the meal. | | | | |
| 15. Server seemed to enjoy job. | | | | |

| | Strongly Agree | Agree | Disagree | Strongly Disagree |
|---|---|---|---|---|
| 16. Server did an excellent job. | | | | |
| Comments: _____ _____ _____ _____ _____ _____ | | | | |
| **Cleanliness/Maintenance** | | | | |
| 1. Dining area clean. | | | | |
| 2. Dining table clean, free of crumbs and stains, and in good repair. | | | | |
| 3. Chairs/booth clean, free of any defects including stains and tears. | | | | |
| 4. Flatware clean and free of waterspots. | | | | |
| 5. Glasses clean and free of waterspots. | | | | |
| 6. Dishware clean and free of waterspots. | | | | |
| 7. Napkins clean, free of spots and attractively folded. | | | | |
| 8. Setting allowed guests to comfortably place arms onto table. | | | | |
| 9. Ceiling was clean. | | | | |
| 10. Ceiling fans were on low speed and clean. | | | | |
| 11. Lighting clear, clean, and appropriate for menu reading. | | | | |
| 12. All light fixtures in working condition. | | | | |

| | Strongly Agree | Agree | Disagree | Strongly Disagree |
|---|---|---|---|---|
| 13. Wall, floors, and windows in good condition and clean. | | | | |
| Comments: _____ _____ _____ _____ _____ | | | | |
| **Atmosphere** | | | | |
| 1. Dining room conducive to conversation. | | | | |
| 2. Dining table lighting appropriate. | | | | |
| 3. Music pleasantly distant and peaceful. | | | | |
| 4. Table centerpiece clean and attractive. | | | | |
| 5. Centerpiece did not interrupt guests' vision of each other. | | | | |
| 6. No noticeable kitchen noise. | | | | |
| 7. Staff careful not to drop dishware or make unnecessary noise. | | | | |
| 8. The following was in agreement with dining theme: | | | | |
| a. Decor. | | | | |
| b. Music. | | | | |
| c. Uniforms. | | | | |
| d. Feeling. | | | | |

| | Strongly Agree | Agree | Disagree | Strongly Disagree |
|---|---|---|---|---|
| 9. Plants were in good physical condition and tastefully exhibited. | | | | |
| 10. Experience was more than expected. | | | | |
| Comments:<br><br>_____<br>_____<br>_____<br>_____<br>_____<br>_____ | | | | |
| **Restrooms**<br>1. Guest restrooms clearly marked and easily found. | | | | |
| 2. Entrance door clean and in good repair. | | | | |
| 3. No objectionable odors present. | | | | |
| 4. Lighting adequate and in good working order. | | | | |
| 5. No signs of graffiti or other damage. | | | | |
| 6. Soap, towels, and toiletries adequate and dispensers clean. | | | | |
| 7. Hooks available. | | | | |
| 8. Fresh flowers or plantlife in good condition and tastefully presented. | | | | |
| 9. Sink areas clean and fixtures shiny. | | | | |
| 10. Mirrors clean. | | | | |
| 11. Floor, walls, and ceiling clean and free from damage. | | | | |
| 12. Wall or ceiling vents clean and free from rust. | | | | |

| | Strongly Agree | Agree | Disagree | Strongly Disagree |
|---|---|---|---|---|
| 13. Restroom decor compatible with theme. | | | | |
| 14. Infant changing area clean and in good repair. | | | | |
| Comments: <br><br>_____ <br>_____ <br>_____ <br>_____ <br>_____ | | | | |
| **Public Telephone Area** | | | | |
| 1. Area conveniently located, clean, and in good repair. | | | | |
| 2. Telephone book available and free of defects. | | | | |
| 3. Ashtray and writing ledge clean and in good repair. | | | | |
| Comments: <br><br>_____ <br>_____ <br>_____ <br>_____ <br>_____ | | | | |
| **Food** | | | | |
| 1. Food items corresponded with their menu descriptions and perceived value. | | | | |
| 2. All items ordered were available. | | | | |
| 3. Hot items were served hot. | | | | |
| 4. Cold items were served cold. | | | | |
| 5. Appetizer: <br><br>   a. Looked appetizing. | | | | |

| | Strongly Agree | Agree | Disagree | Strongly Disagree |
|---|---|---|---|---|
| b. Was fresh. | | | | |
| c. Had excellent color. | | | | |
| d. Had excellent flavor. | | | | |
| e. Was seasoned well. | | | | |
| f. Was presented tastefully. | | | | |
| 6. Soup: | | | | |
| a. Looked appetizing. | | | | |
| b. Was fresh. | | | | |
| c. Had excellent color. | | | | |
| d. Had excellent flavor. | | | | |
| e. Was seasoned well. | | | | |
| f. Was presented tastefully. | | | | |
| 7. Bread: | | | | |
| a. Looked appetizing. | | | | |
| b. Was fresh. | | | | |
| c. Had excellent color. | | | | |
| d. Had excellent flavor. | | | | |
| e. Was presented tastefully. | | | | |

| | Strongly Agree | Agree | Disagree | Strongly Disagree |
|---|---|---|---|---|
| 8. Salad: | | | | |
|    a. Looked appetizing. | | | | |
|    b. Was fresh. | | | | |
|    c. Had excellent color. | | | | |
|    d. Had excellent flavor. | | | | |
|    e. Was well-seasoned. | | | | |
|    f. Was presented tastefully. | | | | |
|    g. Had excellent dressing. | | | | |
| 9. Entree: | | | | |
|    a. Looked appetizing. | | | | |
|    b. Was fresh. | | | | |
|    c. Had excellent color. | | | | |
|    d. Had excellent flavor. | | | | |
|    e. Was well-seasoned. | | | | |
|    f. Was neatly plated and presented tastefully. | | | | |
|    g. Was appropriately portioned. | | | | |
|    h. Was of excellent quality. | | | | |
| 10. Vegetable: | | | | |
|    a. Looked appetizing. | | | | |

|  | Strongly Agree | Agree | Disagree | Strongly Disagree |
|---|---|---|---|---|
| b. Was fresh. | | | | |
| c. Had excellent color. | | | | |
| d. Had excellent flavor. | | | | |
| e. Was presented tastefully. | | | | |
| 11. Starch: | | | | |
| a. Looked appetizing. | | | | |
| b. Was fresh. | | | | |
| c. Had excellent color. | | | | |
| d. Had excellent flavor. | | | | |
| e. Was presented tastefully. | | | | |
| 12. Dessert: | | | | |
| a. Looked appetizing. | | | | |
| b. Was fresh. | | | | |
| c. Had excellent color. | | | | |
| d. Had excellent flavor. | | | | |
| e. Was presented tastefully. | | | | |
| 13. Each of food items corresponded with menu description. | | | | |

| | Strongly Agree | Agree | Disagree | Strongly Disagree |
|---|---|---|---|---|
| Comments:<br><br>——————————<br>——————————<br>——————————<br>——————————<br>——————————<br>—————————— | | | | |
| **Departure**<br><br>1. Guest check presented at appropriate time. | | | | |
| 2. Guest check placed in diplomatic location. | | | | |
| 3. Guest check clear and readable. | | | | |
| 4. Guest check correctly reflected what had been served and was totaled correctly. | | | | |
| 5. Server informed you that he/she would return for payment when you were ready. | | | | |
| 6. Server thanked you after receiving your payment. | | | | |
| 7. Server brought your correct change directly from cashier. | | | | |
| 8. Credit card payment properly tabulated and processed. | | | | |
| 9. You received the check stub. | | | | |
| 10. Server again thanked you for coming and said "it was a pleasure to serve you, and please come again." | | | | |
| 11. Staff recognized you at the exit door with a friendly "good evening" comment. | | | | |
| 12. Corridors and staircases were well lighted and departing from dining room comfortable and pleasant. | | | | |

|  | Strongly Agree | Agree | Disagree | Strongly Disagree |
|---|---|---|---|---|
| Comments: <br> _____ <br> _____ <br> _____ <br> _____ <br> _____ <br> _____ |  |  |  |  |

# Appendix

# Alternative Checklist Formats

Blank forms in this Appendix may be duplicated for your personal use.

| Factor | Not Applicable | Status | | | |
|---|---|---|---|---|---|
| | | Acceptable | In Process | Need to Do | Comments |
| | | | | | |
| | | | | | |
| | | | | | |
| | | | | | |
| | | | | | |
| | | | | | |
| | | | | | |
| | | | | | |
| | | | | | |

| Factor | Procedure | | Corrective Action Requirements |
|--------|-----------|------|-------------------------------|
|        | In Place | Not Done | |
|        |          |      |                                |
|        |          |      |                                |
|        |          |      |                                |
|        |          |      |                                |
|        |          |      |                                |
|        |          |      |                                |
|        |          |      |                                |

230

| Factor | Yes | No |
|---|---|---|
|  |  |  |
|  |  |  |
|  |  |  |
|  |  |  |
|  |  |  |
|  |  |  |
|  |  |  |
|  |  |  |
|  |  |  |
|  |  |  |
|  |  |  |

| Factor | In Practice (✓) | | Not Applicable | If "No" (✓) | | | Responsible Person | Compliance Date |
|---|---|---|---|---|---|---|---|---|
| | Yes | No | | Policy Needed | Procedure Needed | Training Needed | | |
| | | | | | | | | |
| | | | | | | | | |
| | | | | | | | | |
| | | | | | | | | |
| | | | | | | | | |
| | | | | | | | | |
| | | | | | | | | |

232

| Factor | I Do This | | If I Want to Do This | | | |
| | Yes | No | What Must I Do First? | When Will I Begin? | Comments |
|---|---|---|---|---|---|
| | | | | | |
| | | | | | |
| | | | | | |
| | | | | | |
| | | | | | |
| | | | | | |
| | | | | | |

| Factor | Factor Utilized | | Training Strategy, If Any, To Be Used |
| --- | --- | --- | --- |
| | Yes | No | |
| | | | |
| | | | |
| | | | |
| | | | |
| | | | |
| | | | |
| | | | |

| Factor | Now Done | Review Needed | Not Relevant | Comments |
|---|---|---|---|---|
|  |  |  |  |  |
|  |  |  |  |  |
|  |  |  |  |  |
|  |  |  |  |  |
|  |  |  |  |  |
|  |  |  |  |  |
|  |  |  |  |  |
|  |  |  |  |  |
|  |  |  |  |  |
|  |  |  |  |  |

| Factor | Impact Upon Supervisor | | | |
|---|---|---|---|---|
| | Done Consistently | Done Sometimes | Not Done | Include in Training |
| | | | | |
| | | | | |
| | | | | |
| | | | | |
| | | | | |
| | | | | |
| | | | | |
| | | | | |
| | | | | |

| Factor | Person (Position) Responsible | Comments (Procedural Changes Needed) |
|---|---|---|
| | | |
| | | |
| | | |
| | | |
| | | |
| | | |
| | | |
| | | |
| | | |
| | | |

| Factor | Improvement Needed | | If "Yes," Improvement Procedures to Be Used |
|---|---|---|---|
| | Yes | No | |
| | | | |
| | | | |
| | | | |
| | | | |
| | | | |
| | | | |
| | | | |
| | | | |
| | | | |
| | | | |

| Factor | Rating | | | | |
|---|---|---|---|---|---|
| | Inadequate | Fair | Acceptable | Good | Exemplary |
| | | | | | |
| | | | | | |
| | | | | | |
| | | | | | |
| | | | | | |
| | | | | | |
| | | | | | |
| | | | | | |
| | | | | | |
| | | | | | |

| Factor | Important | | If "Yes" | |
|---|---|---|---|---|
| | No | Yes | Currently Included | Need |
| | | | | |
| | | | | |
| | | | | |
| | | | | |
| | | | | |
| | | | | |
| | | | | |
| | | | | |
| | | | | |
| | | | | |

| Factor | Relevance | | If High Relevance | | | | Comments |
|--------|-----------|------|-------------------|-----|-----|--------|----------|
| | Low | High | No Action Needed | Need to Learn More | Use in Management Training | Revise Policy/ Procedure | |
| | | | | | | | |
| | | | | | | | |
| | | | | | | | |
| | | | | | | | |
| | | | | | | | |
| | | | | | | | |
| | | | | | | | |

241

| Factor | In Use (√) | Corrective Action Required | | | | | | Assigned To | Compliance Date |
|---|---|---|---|---|---|---|---|---|---|
| | | Develop | | Closer Supervision | Training Needed | Other (Describe) | | | |
| | | Procedure | Policy | | | | | | |
| | | | | | | | | | |
| | | | | | | | | | |
| | | | | | | | | | |
| | | | | | | | | | |
| | | | | | | | | | |
| | | | | | | | | | |

| Factor | Status | | |
|---|---|---|---|
| | Not Applicable | Is Being Done | Must Begin to Do |
| | | | |
| | | | |
| | | | |
| | | | |
| | | | |
| | | | |
| | | | |
| | | | |
| | | | |
| | | | |

243

| Factor | C | TC | NC | NA | Comments |
|--------|---|----|----|----|----------|
|        |   |    |    |    |          |
|        |   |    |    |    |          |
|        |   |    |    |    |          |
|        |   |    |    |    |          |
|        |   |    |    |    |          |
|        |   |    |    |    |          |
|        |   |    |    |    |          |
|        |   |    |    |    |          |
|        |   |    |    |    |          |

C = Compliance, TC = Toward Compliance, NC = Noncompliance, NA = Not Applicable